COMPUTER GRAPHICS

118 Computer-Generated Designs

by
MELVIN L. PRUEITT

Staff Member, Los Alamos Scientific Laboratory
of the University of California

Dover Publications, Inc., New York

Published in Canada by General Publishing Company, Ltd., 30 Lesmill Road, Don Mills, Toronto, Ontario.
Published in the United Kingdom by Constable and Company, Ltd., 10 Orange Street, London WC 2.

Computer Graphics: 118 Computer-Generated Designs is a new work, first published by Dover Publications, Inc., in 1975.
The research and illustrations contained in this book were performed under the auspices of the United States Atomic Energy Commission.

DOVER *Pictorial Archive* SERIES

International Standard Book Number: 0-486-23178-X
Library of Congress Catalog Card Number: 74-18611

Manufactured in the United States of America
Dover Publications, Inc.
180 Varick Street
New York, N.Y. 10014

INTRODUCTION

Until the present, the artist has worked by hand and eye. Today, however, man may conceive form and color for machines to translate into reality. The modern electronic computer can deftly control an electron beam and camera or manipulate a pen over paper to generate designs appealing to man. Some of these designs are simple; others make elaborate use of perspective. This book represents a sampling of such designs.

Because an artist has traditionally been defined as a creative person with sufficient hand-eye coordination to produce art, some critics would contend that computer-generated art is not art at all since the artist is not in intimate contact with his creation. But what about the individual who is deeply moved by a work of art or a view of nature's artistry and hasn't the skill to reproduce what he sees? He might be defined as a "passive artist," for he recreates within himself what he sees. He is able to relate emotionally to the color and form of the image he has generated in his mind—the image of an external object. In this sense, the passive artist may be superior to some professional artists who have the technical skill to create, but lack an emotional relationship with their creations.

The computer has brought in the day of the passive artist. It may make art possible for him; it does not make it easy. The artist may conceive of eloquent designs, but he must face the difficult task of instructing the computer to duplicate his conceptions. Computer programs are the tools that perform most of the operations in the production of computer art. Although they are invaluable in easing the difficulty of transforming the idea into the actual picture, the artist must be able to communicate his designs to the computer in terms of numbers or mathematical functions. Thus, computer art is in many ways far more difficult than other, more traditional, forms of art.

Some computer art consists of abstract lines on a two-dimensional surface, but there are computer programs that can create "three-dimensional" images. These are not, of course, actually three-dimensional, but by some logic network, the human brain transforms drawings in perspective into objects in the round. Consider the familiar "optical illusion" stairway which seems to invert itself periodically as the brain attempts to order an ambiguity. (In Figs. 69 and 70, both an isometric and a perspective plot of a stairway are drawn. The isometric plot is ambiguous; the perspective plot is not.)

The mathematics involved in teaching a computer to draw in perspective is relatively simple. Given a set of numbers which defines the positions of a set of

INTRODUCTION

points in space, one merely needs to "project" the points mathematically onto an imaginary screen. These points are represented by numbers that are transmitted to a plotting device for the generation of the image of the points and the lines that connect them. But *all* the points and lines end up on the plotted image, even the lines which should be hidden behind other features of the image. Compare Fig. 1 and Fig. 2. Many researchers have found that the problem of removing the superfluous lines—the "hidden-line problem"—does not have a simple solution. Most hidden-line removal programs consume far too much computer time to be used extensively.

PICTURE, a computer program which I developed at the Los Alamos Scientific Laboratory, constitutes a fast algorithm for plotting arrays of numbers in perspective with hidden lines removed. Although the program is designed primarily to display mathematical functions and experimental data, it also generates aesthetic forms in the hands of a designer. Once an array of numbers has been delivered to the program and a viewpoint specified, the program, in the framework of the computer, performs rotation, projection and hidden-line removal. This is all done in terms of numbers. Nothing remotely resembling an image is developed until the numbers, in the form of electronic pulses, reach a plotting device.

In order to produce a visual representation of a set of numbers which gives the illusion of a surface, PICTURE first generates a regular rectangular grid of lines. It is important that the grid lines be regularly spaced. Irregular spacing interferes with the ability of the human brain to interpret properly complex computer productions. The intersections of the grid lines of this two-dimensional mesh are then raised in the third dimension to heights that are proportional to the function which is to be represented over the surface. The computer could not actually present this three-dimensional form to man for observation unless it were to carve the function from a solid block, but it can do almost as well by producing a picture in perspective, which creates the illusion of three dimensions. This is done mathematically by projecting the grid lines of the surface onto an imaginary image screen placed between the viewer and the surface. The line of sight from the viewer's eye to the intersection of two grid lines strikes the image screen at a point that becomes the intersection image. After all the intersections and connecting lines are cast onto the image screen, the image is in perspective.

What lines on the image screen should be hidden? Since there is no depth to the screen, the computer "sees" only a mass of lines on a two-dimensional surface—none are behind any others. We must go back to the rectangular grid to calculate the distance of lines from the viewpoint. Starting from the closest line on the grid and working away, the computer program compares the corresponding lines on the image screen. If a distant line is lower than a nearer line along a common line of sight, it is hidden. If the distant line is higher than all the lines between it and the viewer, it is visible. When a line is partially higher and partially lower than a nearer line, the intersection of the two is calculated and the former is cut to the appropriate length. By inverting the whole array the bottom surface may be treated similarly.

PICTURE has the options of adding a transparent box around the figure to aid the eye in judging sizes, labeling X, Y, and Z axes and the origin, placing numbers to the left of the box to show the size of the box, and drawing lines (called side bars) from the edge of the surface to the base of the box. When side bars on the viewer's side are requested, the program automatically removes all lines from the bottom of the surface.

Color adds beauty to an image, but it also has the practical value of making the various parts of a complex form more distinguishable. The top of the surface, the side bars, and the box may all be different colors. Seven colors (including white) may be generated by mounting three complementary color filters, controlled electrically by the computer, between the cathode-ray tube and the camera. With four colors per picture and seven colors to choose from, 840 different color combinations are possible.

The number of color combinations may be increased by using a PICTURE option which defines the portion of the surface to be plotted. Then the color may be changed and another portion plotted. Thus checkerboards, stripes and other patterns are easily created. Color changes may be made according to heights of the function, which also allows the deletion of portions of the image. The designer's imagination is staggered by the possibilities presented by this large number of variables. After conceiving a form from among the infinite number of different shapes and translating the geometry into numbers, he must still choose colors and patterns. At what angle and inclination should it be viewed? From how far? How should the side bars be treated? How fine a grid should be used? Are lines running only in the X direction more suitable than lines running in both directions?

I sometimes allow the computer to choose the colors by means of a numerical random number generator. That eases the load of decision making when a large number of varied plots are to be made, but the color combinations are not always good. This illustrates the value of the computer in art. When the ordinary artist paints a scene, he may ask, "I wonder how it would look if the viewpoint were on the other side," or "How would it look if I used different colors?" He can find out only by considerable effort of repainting. The computer can produce, from a single array of numbers, images from a variety of angles and with different color combinations. The designer can then select his favorite.

There is still a gap between the designer's concept and the realization of the picture. It is the designer's responsibility to choose (or derive) the functions which can define his mental creation. He must formulate his ideas in the language of the computer—numbers. It is possible to punch all the numbers of an array into cards and read them into the computer, but that is laborious (a 50 x 50 array contains 2,500 points). It is easier to produce a simple computer calling program which first determines the numbers in repetitive loops and then calls the plotting program. The calling program uses mathematical functions to provide smooth curves.

The pictures that fill this book are visual representations of sets of numbers. Most of them resulted from the deliberate intention to create a particular form. Some turned out to be surprises when the result did not match the original conception. A few were errors. Some, near the end, resulted from the plotting of data from nature—experimental data. Even the heart of the atom—the nucleus—revealed some of its secrets in Figs. 99–102. The computer "con-

INTRODUCTION

ceived" Figs. 37–50, which were the offspring of pseudo-random numbers. But even here, the characteristics of the "random plots" were determined by man. These pictures were the summation of several bivariate normal distribution functions. The number of the functions and the width, height and position of each function were determined randomly, but the limits on these numbers and the type of function had to be set by man.

In many cases the array is displayed in different manners or with different viewing angles in more than one sequential figure. In some figures, we may note distortion resulting from a very close viewpoint. The computer viewpoint is moved down below the surface in some instances to give the observer a look at features which may be hidden when viewed from above. These are not "computer-eye" views, of course, because the computer deals blindly in numbers only.

We may marvel at the gentle flow of form and the color combinations of the surfaces or the rugged prominences of the images on the following pages, but these images are the progeny of what is perhaps a far more magnificent beauty —the beauty of a logic system. The computer program consists of a set of instructions which forms an intricate logic network designed to guide the computer in the performance of desired tasks. This beauty is seldom observed by anyone but the programmer himself, who is often exhilarated by inventing a unique twist in the complexities of logic, but cannot show the beauty of his invention to others because they cannot usually appreciate the whole. He must be resigned to view his creation alone. Only the fruits of a program such as PICTURE may be appreciated by others. It seems almost miraculous that, given any two-dimensional array of numbers, this program can create a perspective plot with hidden lines removed in exactly the right places even though it has never before "seen" that particular array of numbers. It is the complex logic system of the computer program that makes such pictures possible.

And finally there is the greatest logic system of them all—the human brain —which allows us to observe a set of lines on a sheet of paper and to envisage a three-dimensional form. This is the logic system that takes different wavelengths of light, different photon energies, and presents color to our awareness. This is the system which can tie together a sequence of static pictures isolated at points of time and award us a sense of motion. With this tool we are equipped to bridge the gap in communications left by the computer as it scrawled its lines upon a surface from the numbers the computer had thought.

Los Alamos
November, 1974

MELVIN L. PRUEITT

COMPUTER GRAPHICS

118 Computer-Generated Designs

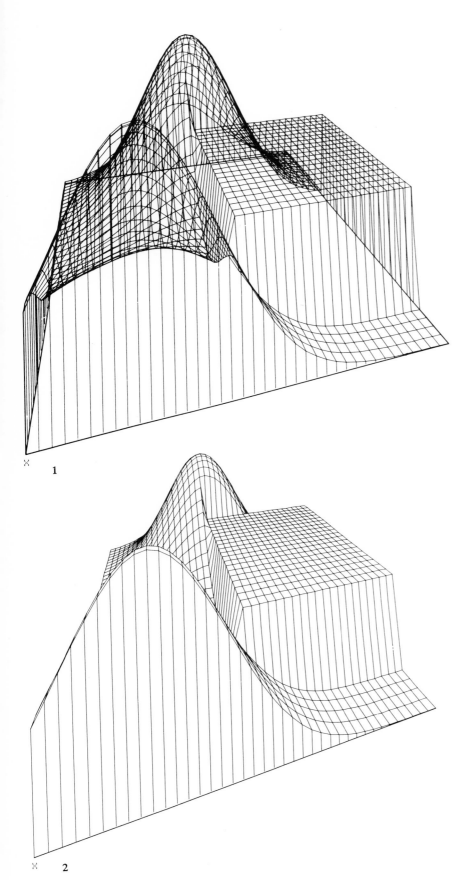

1, 2. Hidden-line removal. The value of removing lines which should be hidden if the figure is to appear to be in the round is made apparent by comparing Figure 1, which contains hidden lines, with Figure 2, in which the hidden lines have been removed. The human visual system can quickly assess the scene represented in Figure 2, but Figure 1 causes confusion.

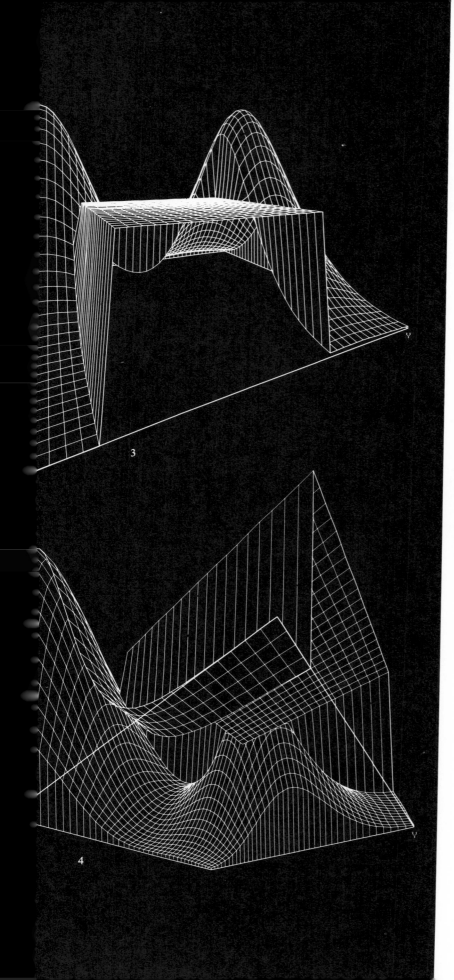

3, 4. The same array as in Figure 1, plotted from different angles. Figure 4 provides a view from below. These arrays were generated by adding a bivariate normal distribution function $F\ (X,Y) = C \exp\left\{-\left[(X-X_1)^2 + (Y-Y_1)^2\right]/W\right\}$ at two different places and a step function.

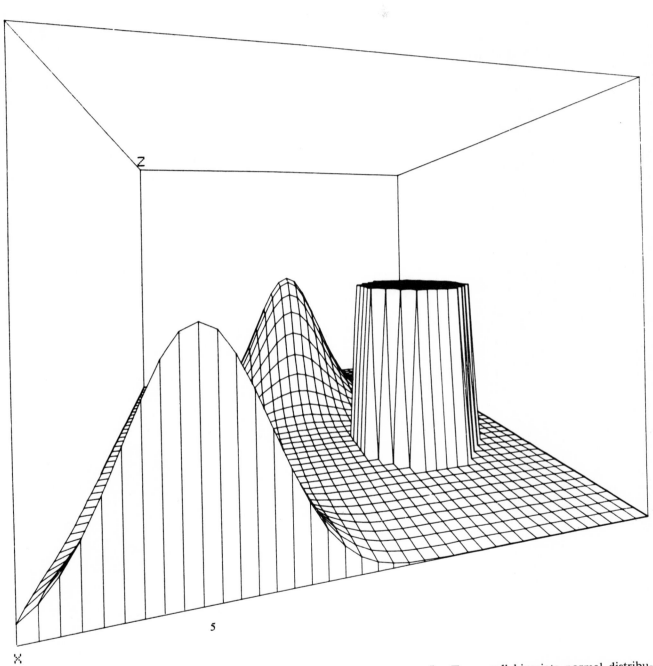

5. Two small bivariate normal distribution functions and a cylindrical column. The transparent "box" drawn around the plotting space helps the eye to judge distance and size. The X and Z axes of the coordinate system are labeled in the figure; the Y axis is invisible in this plot.

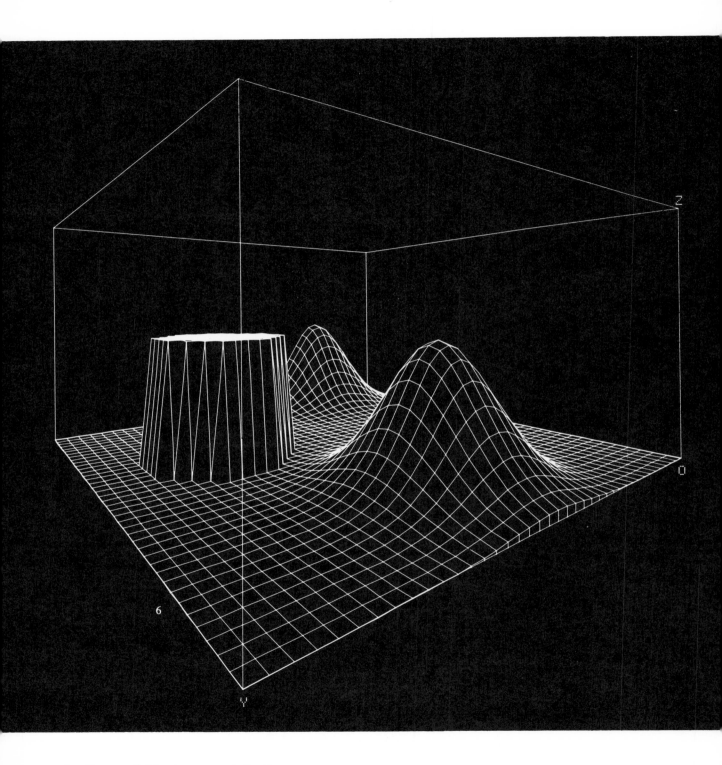

6. Two small bivariate normal distribution functions and a cylindrical column. The column is not perfectly circular because of the coarseness of the mesh.

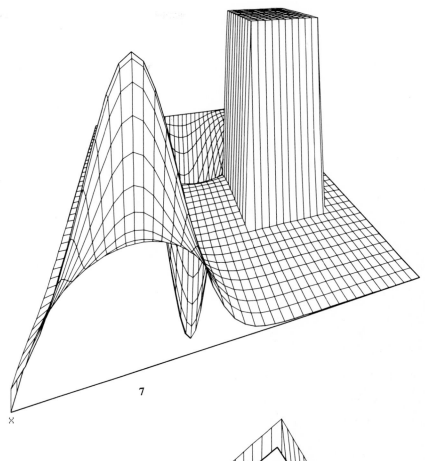

7

7, 8. A positive and a negative bivariate normal distribution function with a rectangular column (Fig. 7) viewed from above. Figure 8 shows the same array as Figure 7, but rotated and viewed from below.

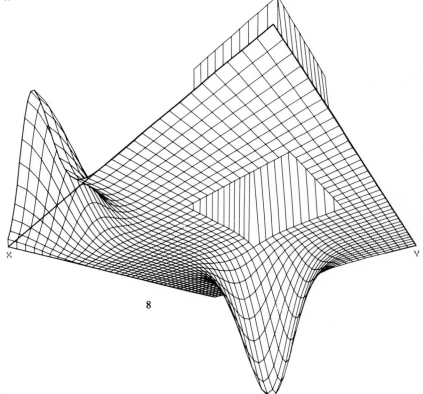

8

5

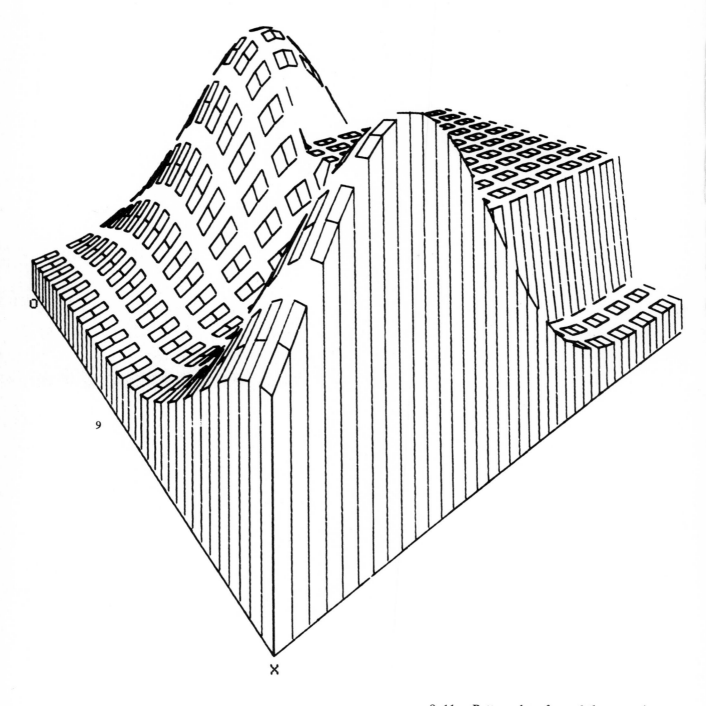

9–11. Patterned surface of the array in Figure 1. Different patterns on the same plot can be used to differentiate various areas.

10

11

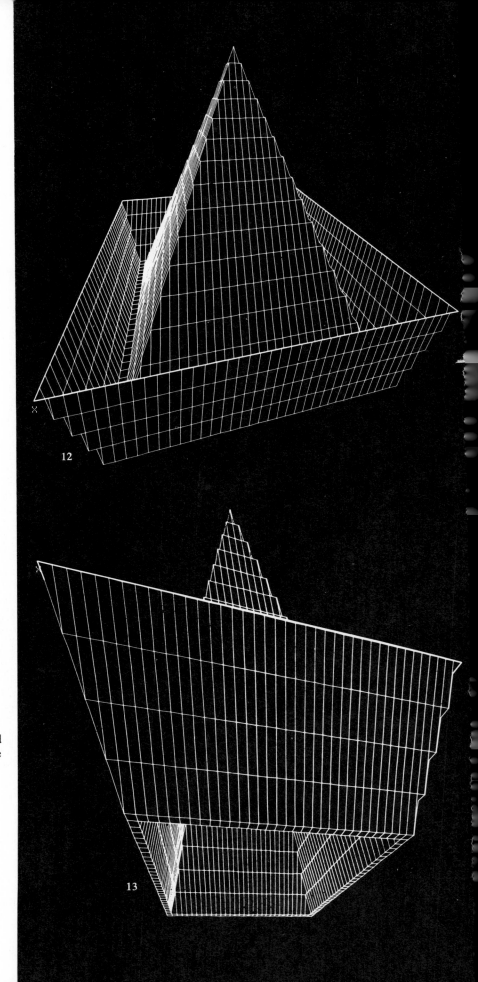

12, 13. Sunken pyramid, constructed from a set of intersecting planes. Figure 13 is viewed from below.

8

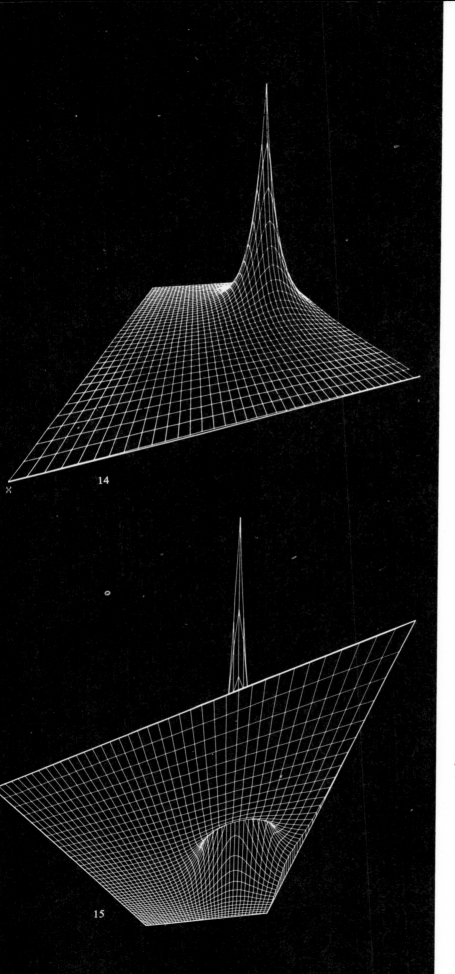

14, 15. Spires. Exponential decay
$F(X,Y) = C \, \exp \left\{ -(|X - X_1| - |Y - Y_1|) \middle/ W \right\}$.

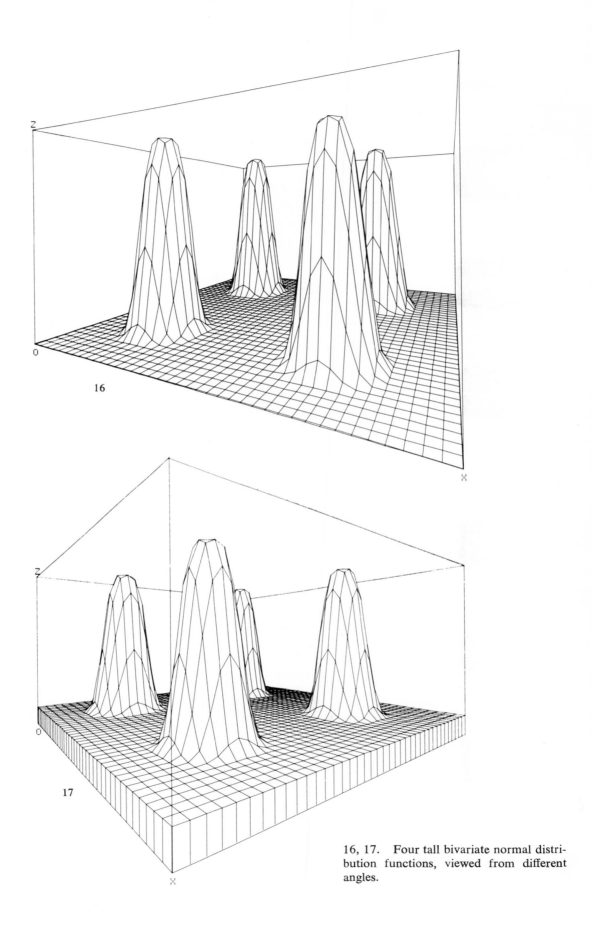

16

17

16, 17. Four tall bivariate normal distribution functions, viewed from different
angles.

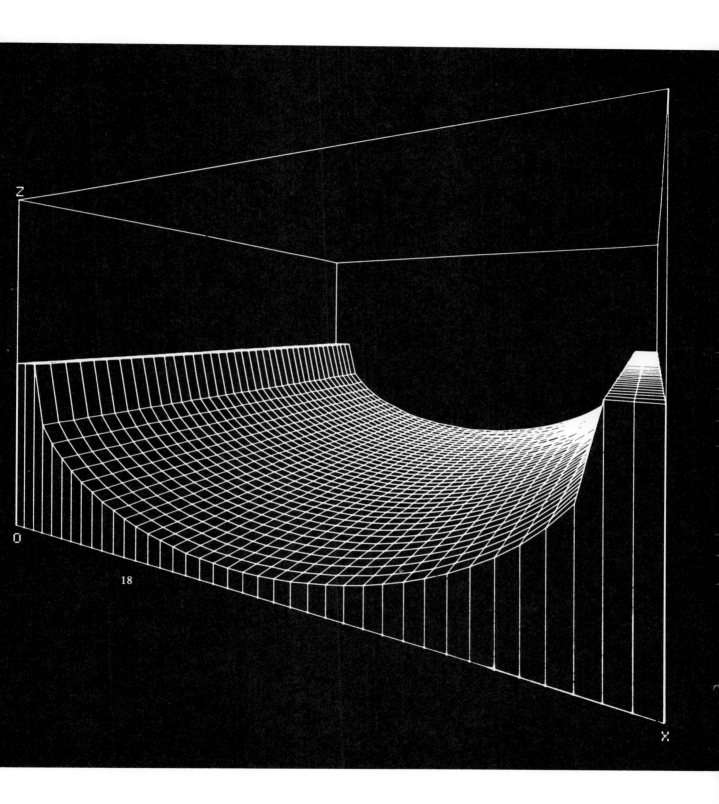

18. Lower half of a cylinder. When the
computer is instructed to fill the frame
with the plot, distortion sometimes oc-
curs. This cylinder is slightly flattened as
a result of such distortion.

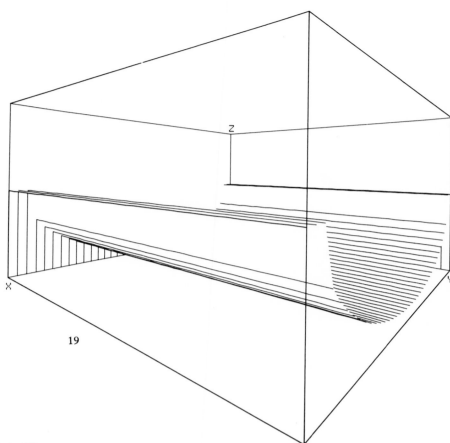

19

19. Lower half of a cylinder.
20. Dome. $F = A - B [(X - C)^2 + (Y - C)^2]$ where F defines the array of numbers.

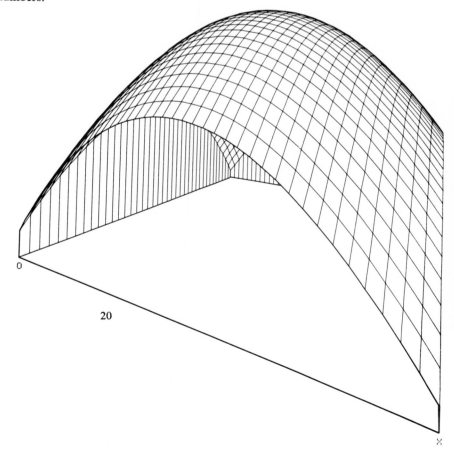

20

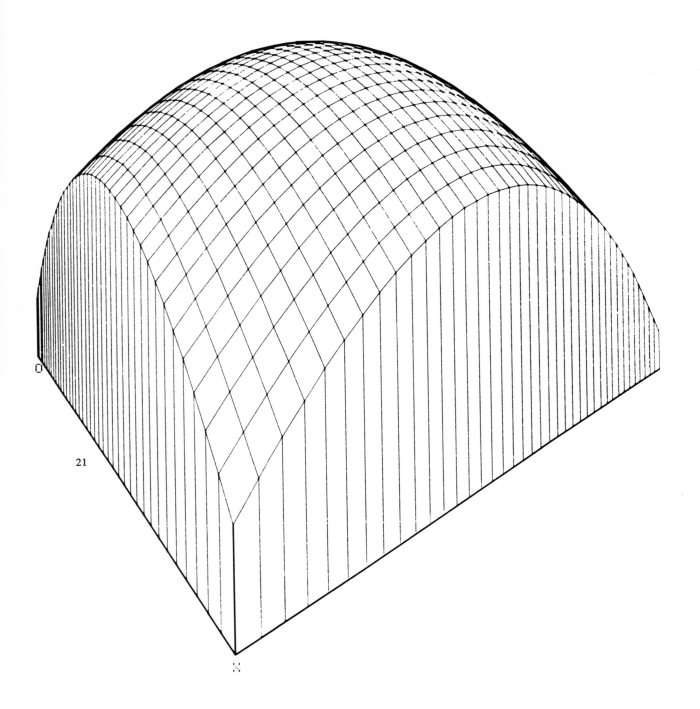

21

21. Another view of Figure 20. By placing the side bars on the near edges of the surface, and by eliminating the underside, the impression is made that the object is solid.

22, 23.   Rectangular columns created by raising sets of points to various heights.

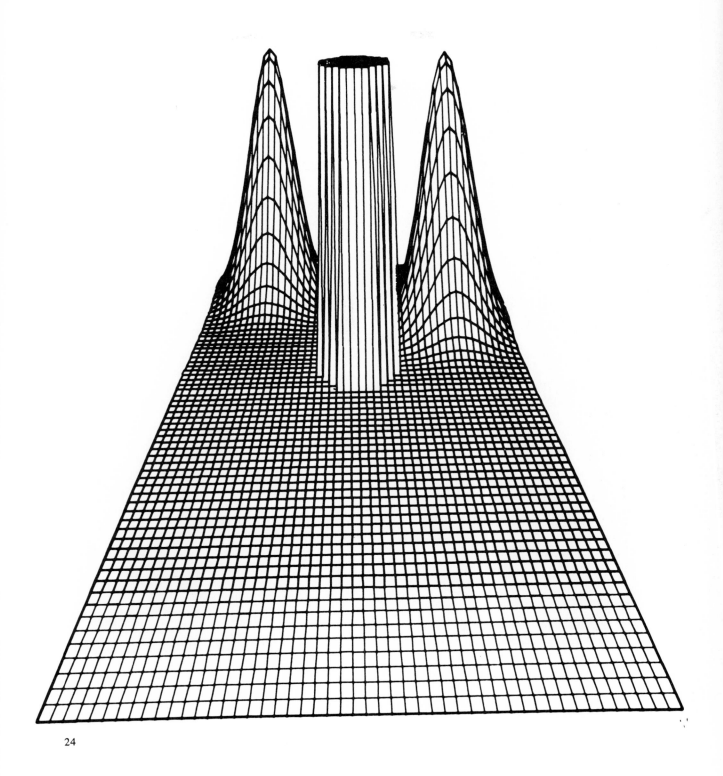

24

24. A close viewpoint creates a strong sense of perspective.

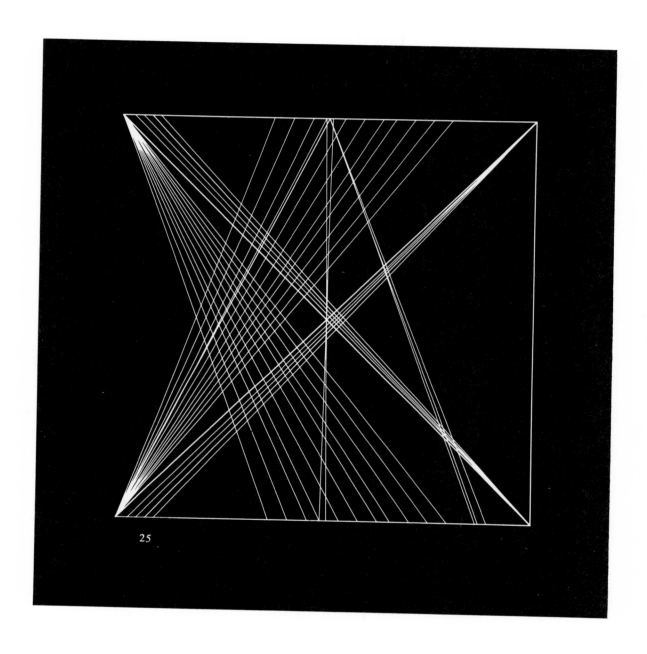

25. An error. The source of error can be human, it can be in the computer, which occasionally has an electronic failure, or it can be in the plotter, which may have difficulty reading the computer-produced magnetic tape.

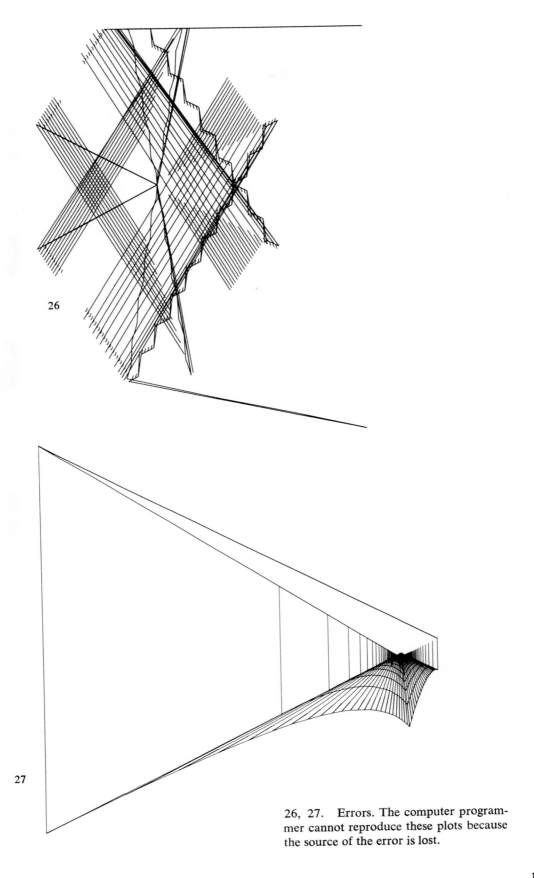

26, 27.   Errors. The computer programmer cannot reproduce these plots because the source of the error is lost.

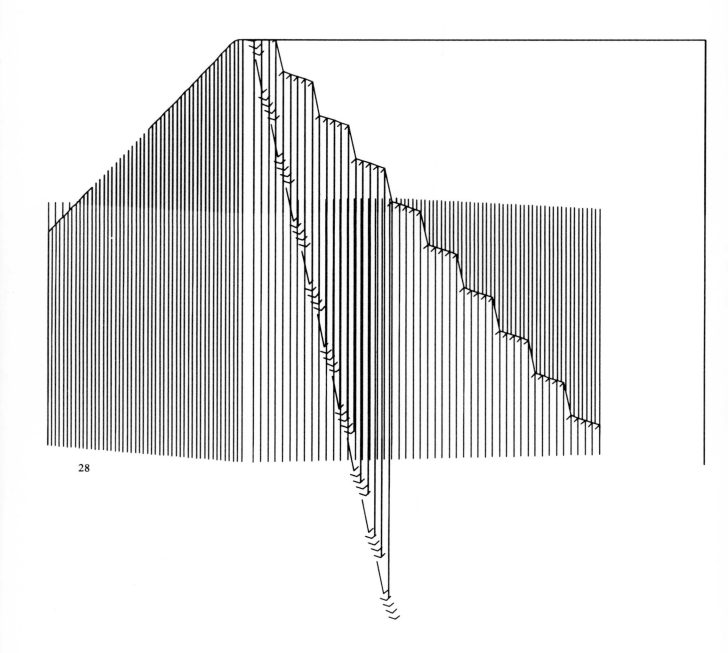

28

28–31. Errors.

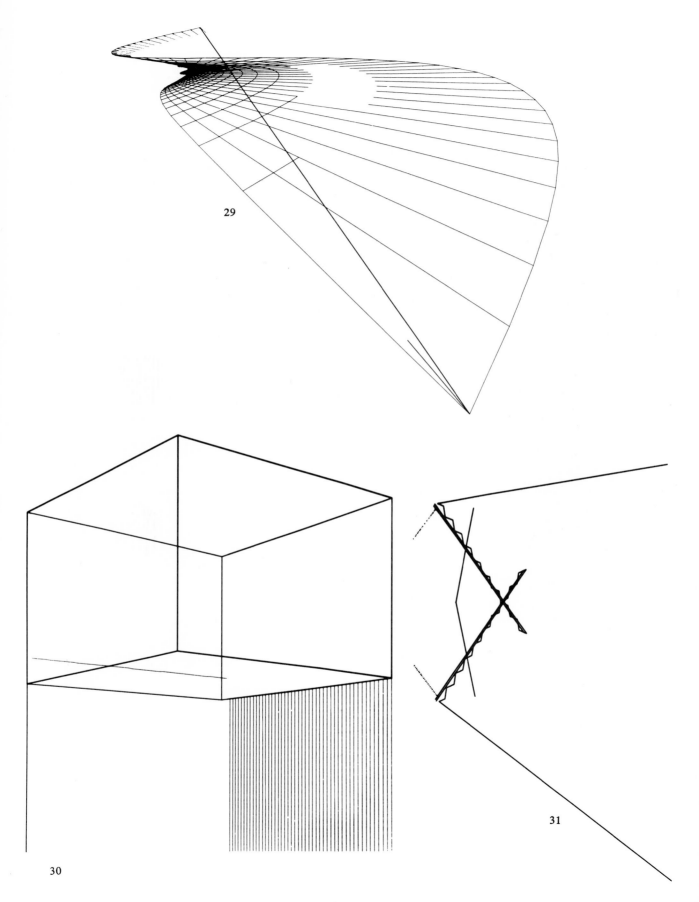

29

30

31

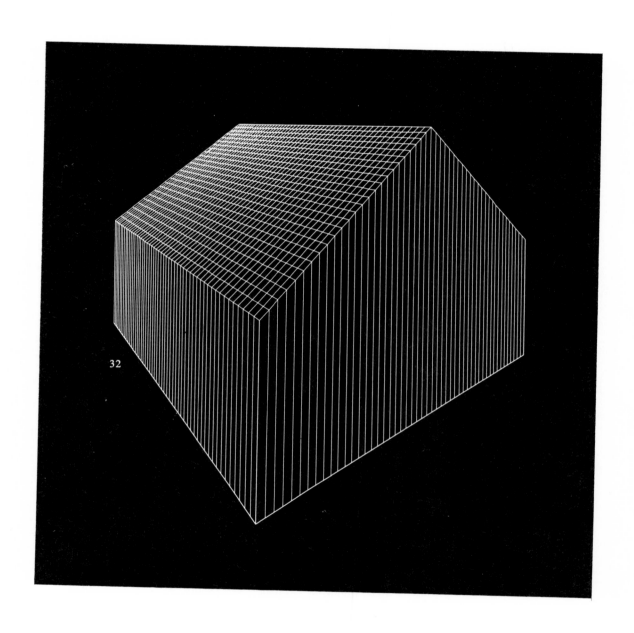

32. The roof of this house was formed
by two intersecting planes. The walls
were formed by side bars.

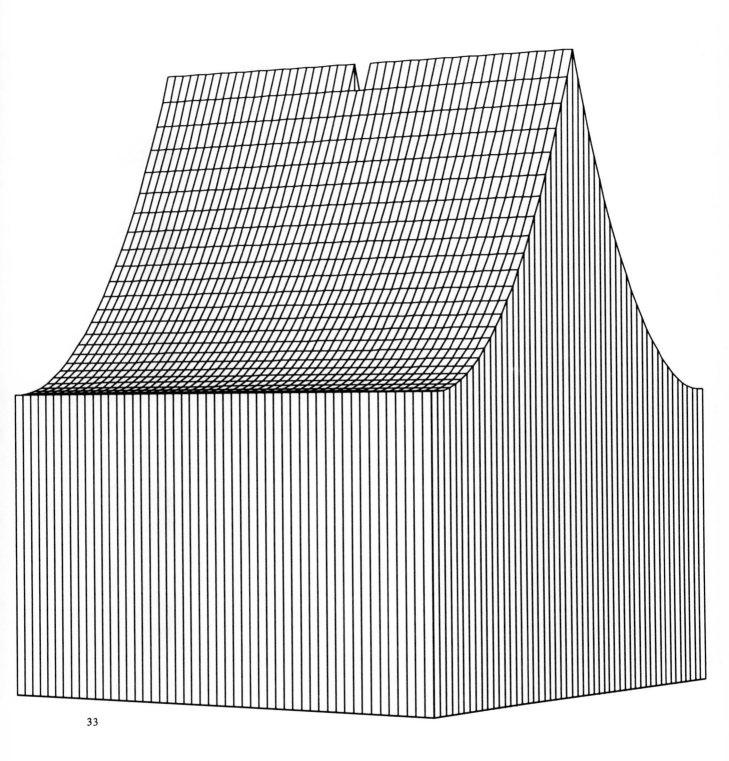

33

33. The roof of this house was formed when an equation was not properly specified.

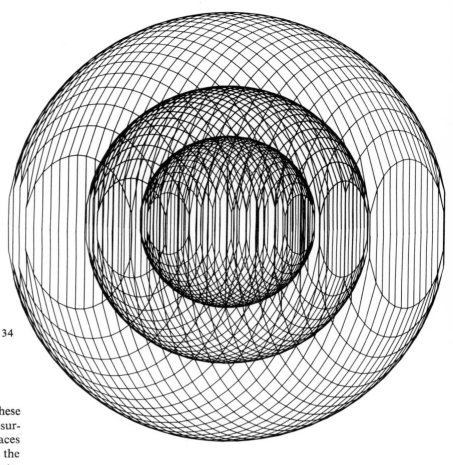

34

34–36. Concentric spheres. These spheres are paradoxical—their front surfaces are opaque to their back surfaces (i.e., the back cannot be seen), but the front surfaces are transparent to the interior spheres. This is made apparent in Figure 36, where some of the connecting lines have been omitted. One cannot see the back surface of the sphere. Figure 35 has lines running in only one direction.

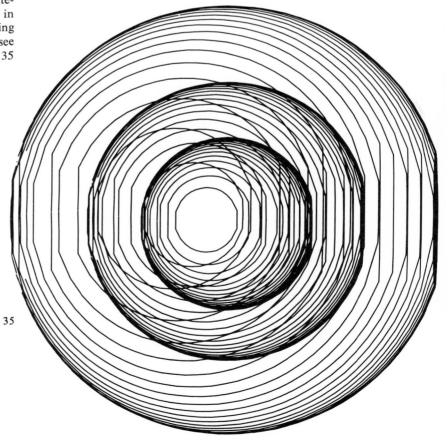

35

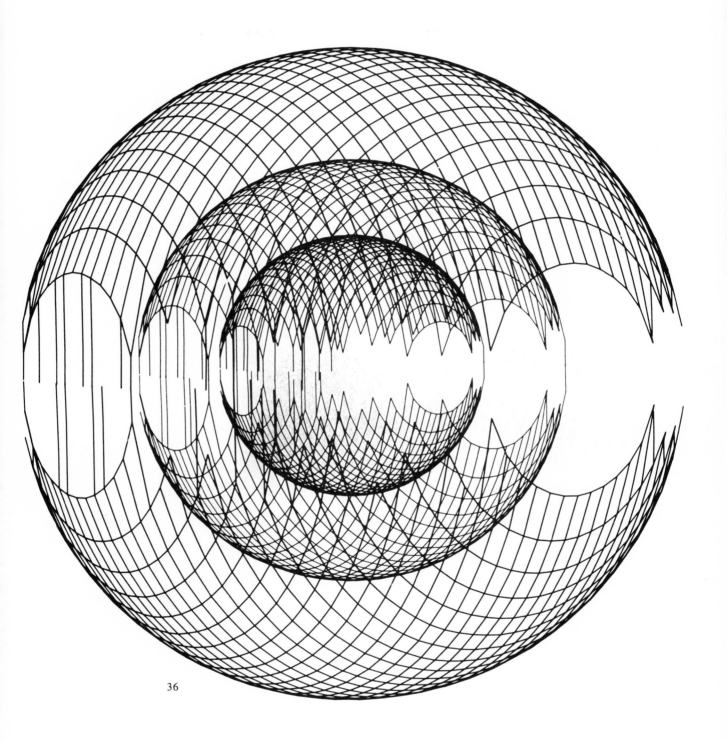

36

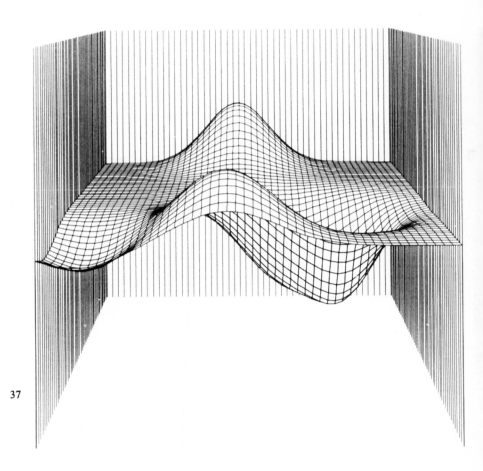

37

37–39. The superposition of bivariate
normal distribution functions with positions, widths and amplitudes chosen randomly. This might be called true computer art; the computer arranged the lay-
out of the functions by generating random numbers which specified the positions and sizes of the features.

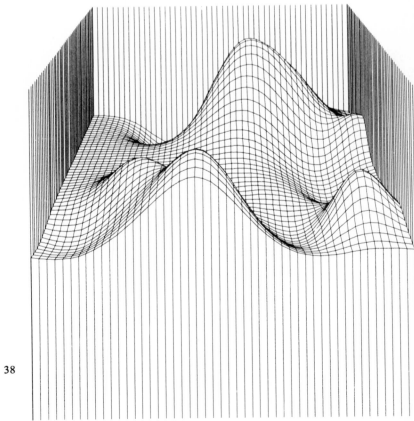

38

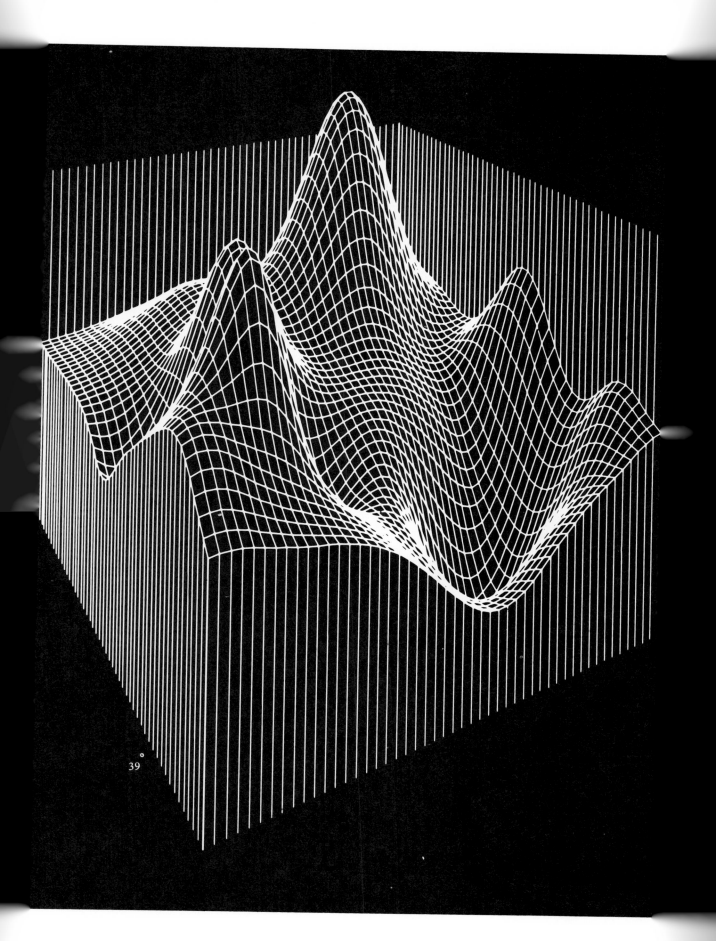

39

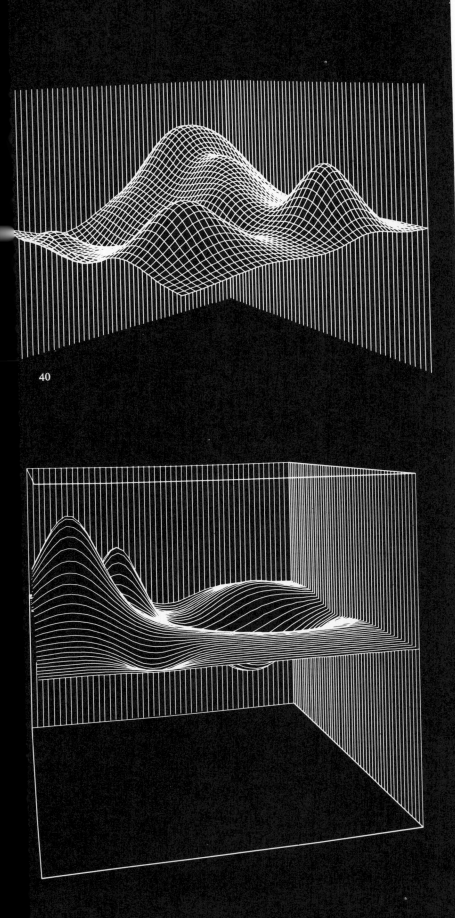

40

40–42. Bivariate normal distribution fuctions with positions, widths and amplitudes chosen randomly. Note the effects created by different arrangements of the side bars.

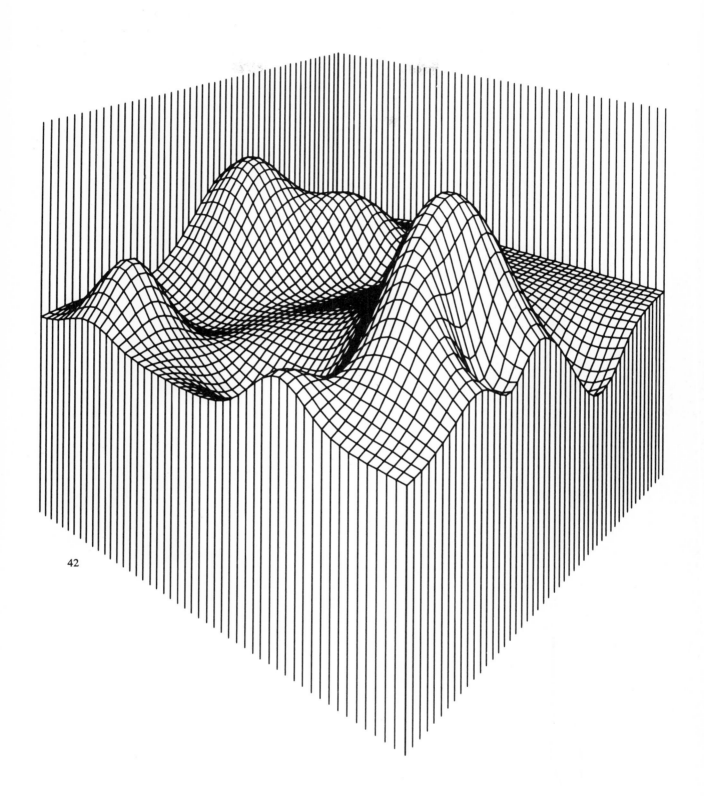

42

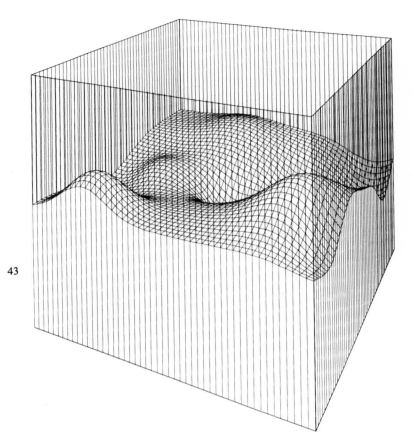

43

43–45. Bivariate normal distribution functions with positions, widths and amplitudes chosen randomly. Figures 43 and 44 show the effect of transparent side bars placed on the near edges of the surface. The plot of Figure 45 was cropped by the computer.

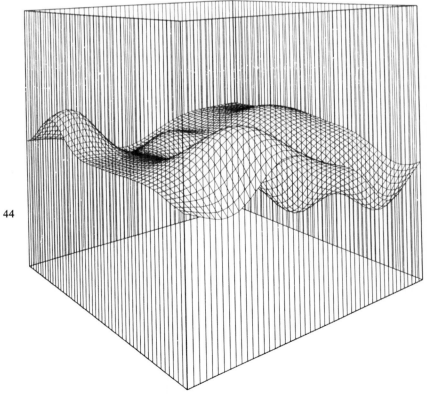

44

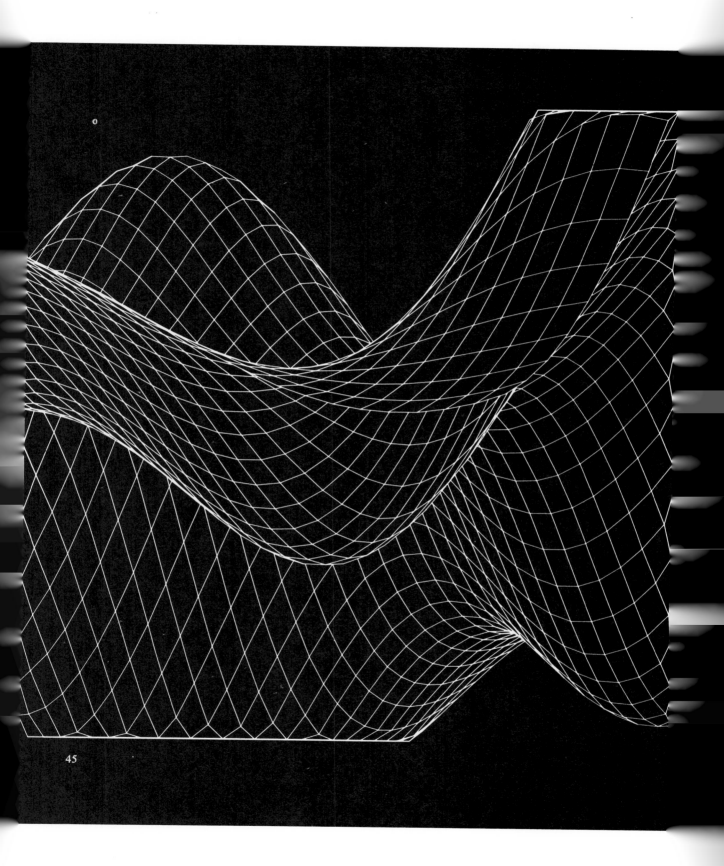

45

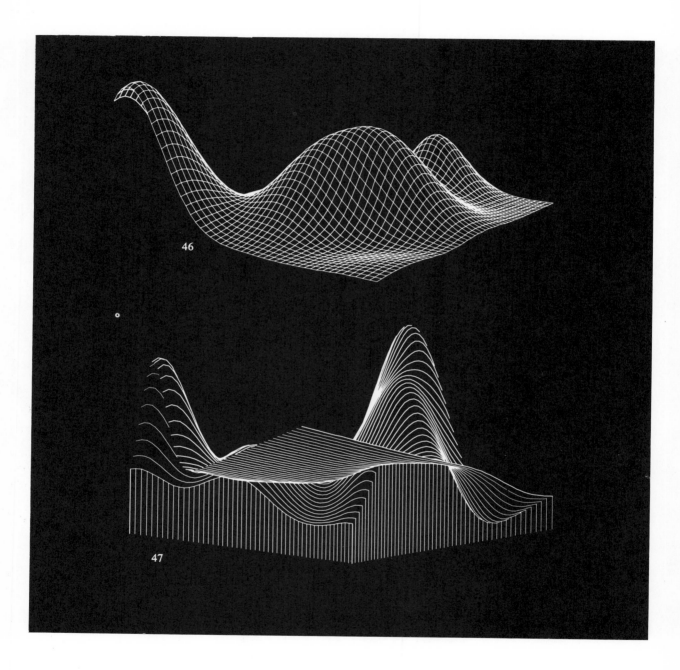

46–48. Bivariate normal distribution functions with positions, widths and amplitudes chosen randomly. Sometimes a design is more esthetically appealing when lines are plotted in only one direction (Fig. 47). In Figure 48, very rugged features are produced simply by specifying large amplitudes for the functions.

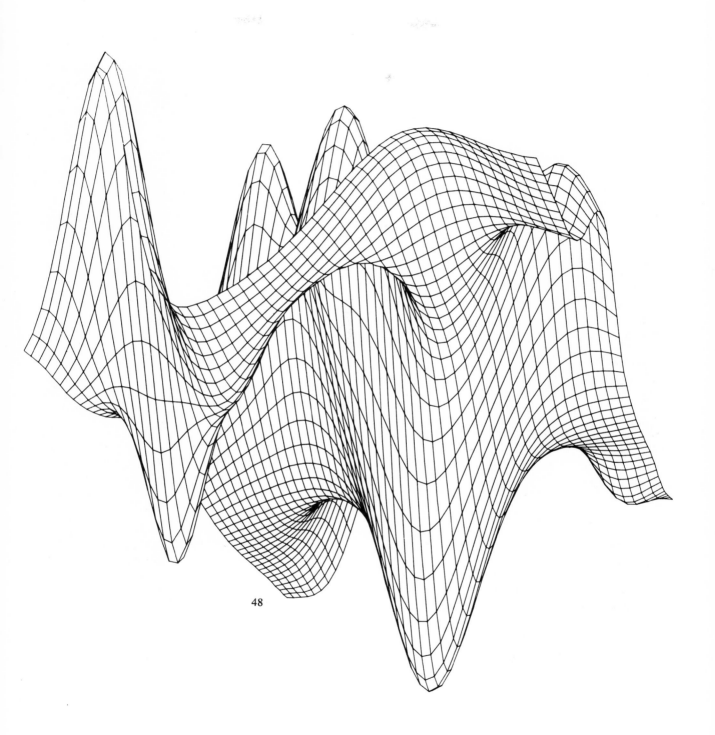

48

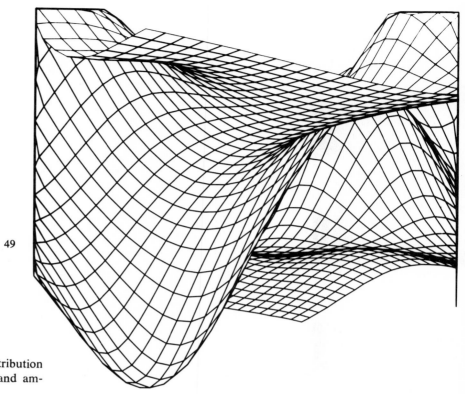

49

49, 50. Bivariate normal distribution functions with positions, widths and amplitudes chosen randomly.

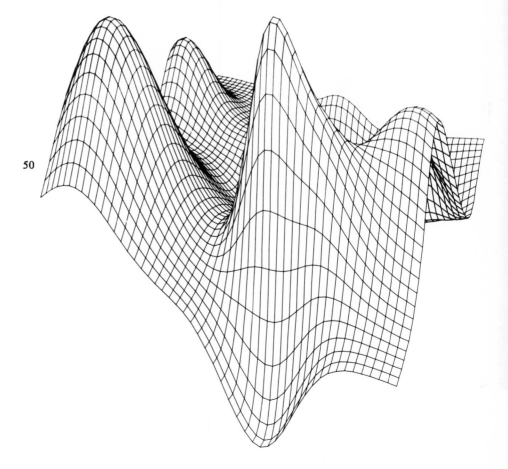

50

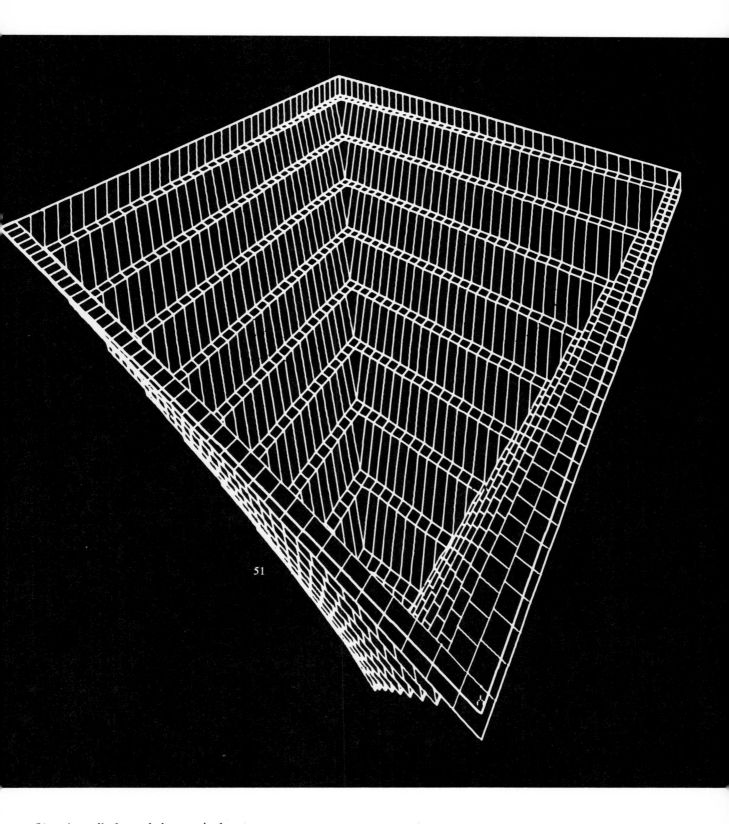

51. A well formed by a single step
which spirals down to the vertex.

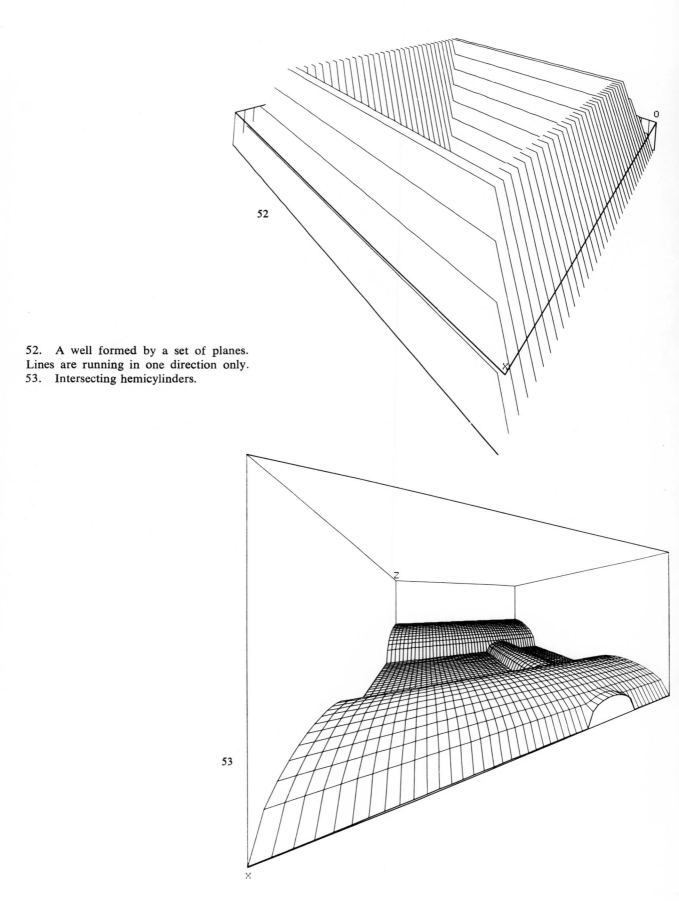

52. A well formed by a set of planes.
Lines are running in one direction only.
53. Intersecting hemicylinders.

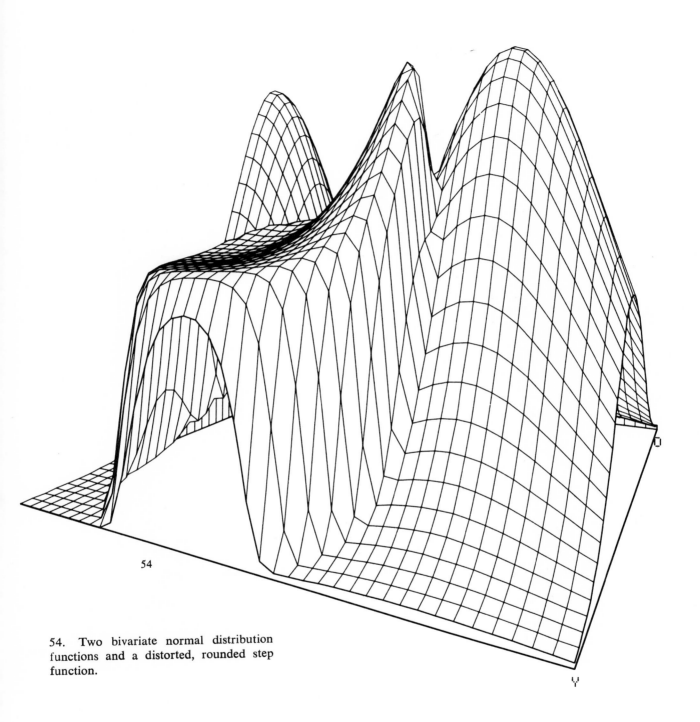

54

54. Two bivariate normal distribution functions and a distorted, rounded step function.

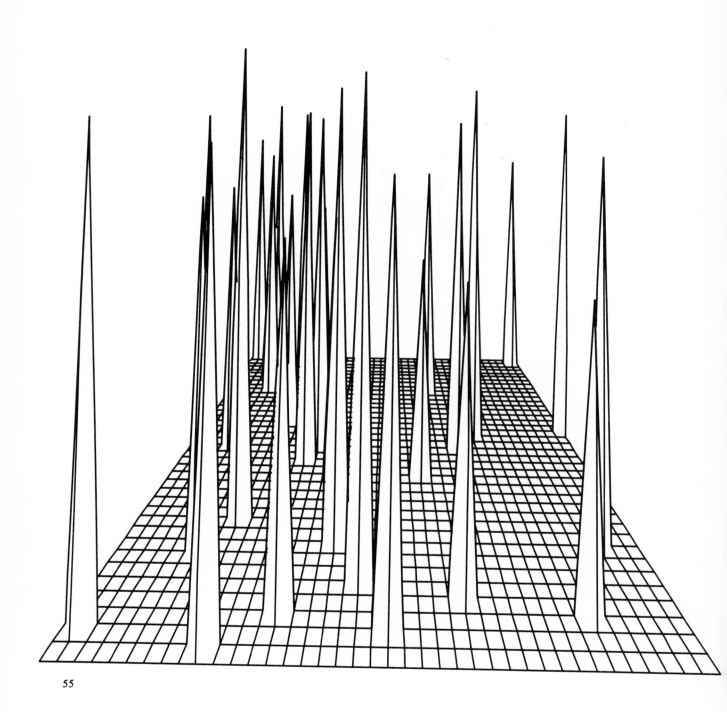

55

55. Random points with random heights. Most of the points were set to zero by the computer, which then chose points randomly to set to random values.

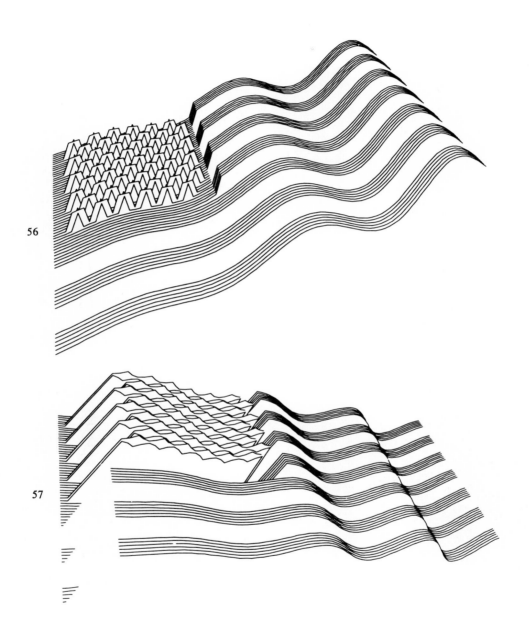

56, 57. U.S. flags in relief. The lines
run in one direction. The flag's white
stripes are made by lowering some of the
lines so that they become hidden.

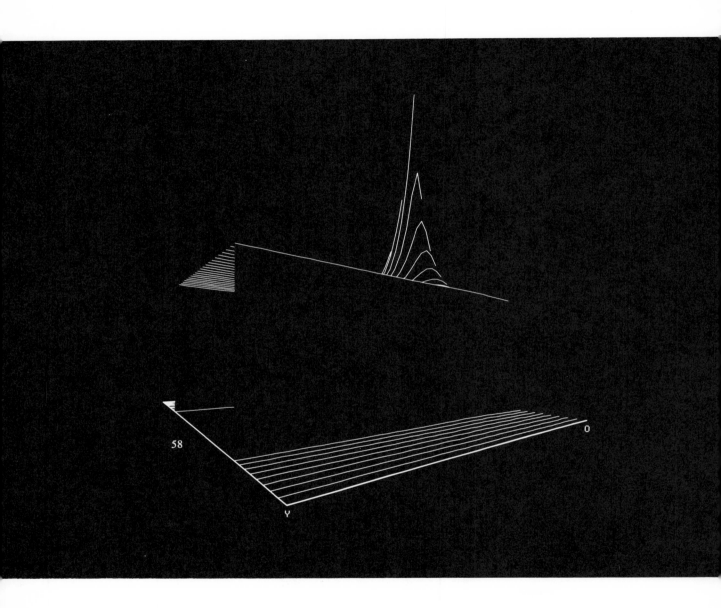

58. Cathedral. The surface was formed
by adding a step function and an exponential decay function. Even when full
visual information is lacking, the human
optical system attempts to reconstruct an
object and, although it is not drawn, the
nearer wall seems to be present.

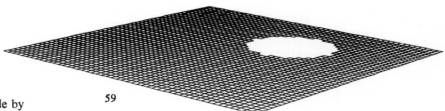

59

59. Hemisphere above a plane, made by leaving out the lines of the column which connect the plane to the hemisphere.

60. Close-up of a sphere connected to figures of rotation. The side of the sphere appears to be flattened because of the coarseness of the mesh.

60

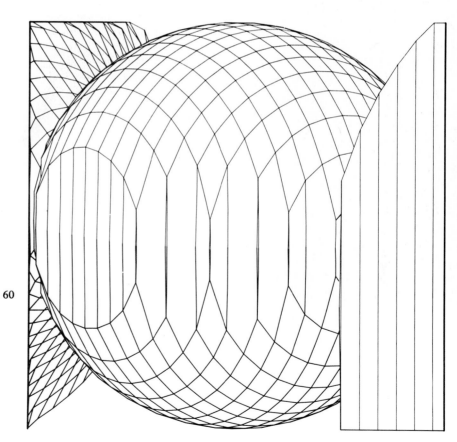

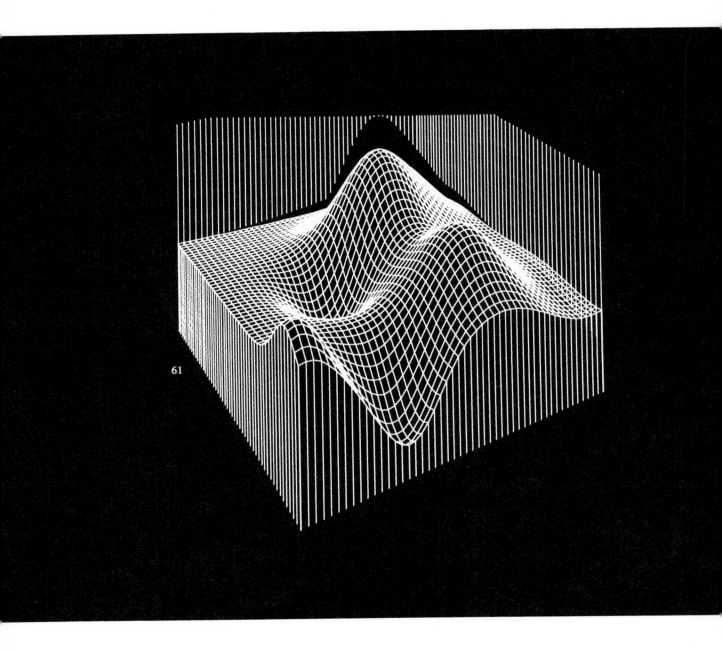

61. Mountain shadow. The effect was
created by shifting the background side
bars.

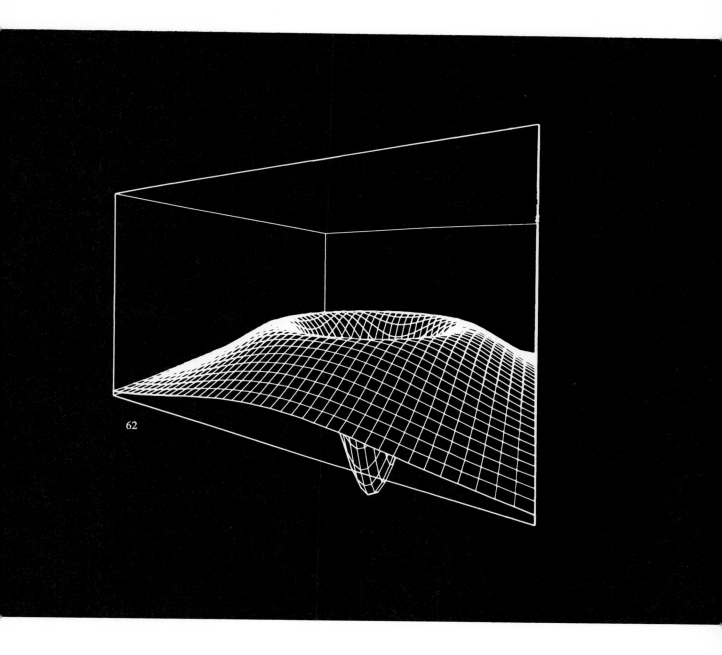

62. Concentric error functions. A negative and a positive two-dimensional error function added together create a volcano effect. The negative error function is narrower than the positive function but has a coefficient with a larger magnitude.

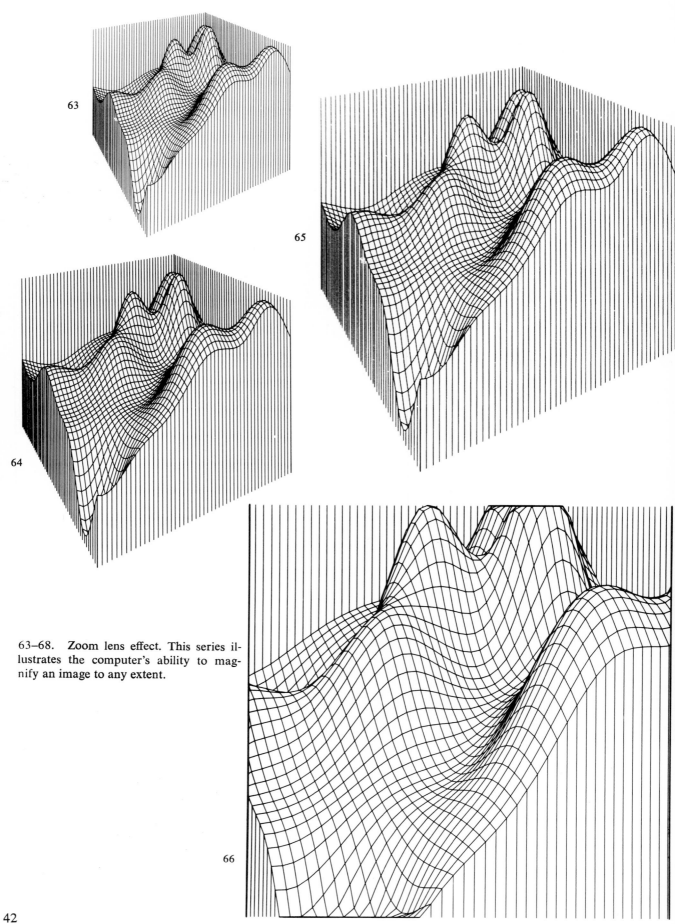

63–68. Zoom lens effect. This series illustrates the computer's ability to magnify an image to any extent.

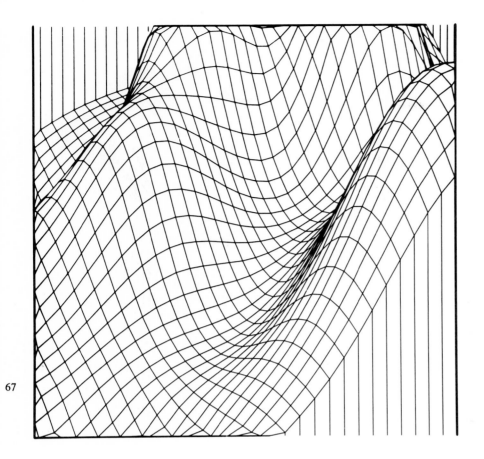

67

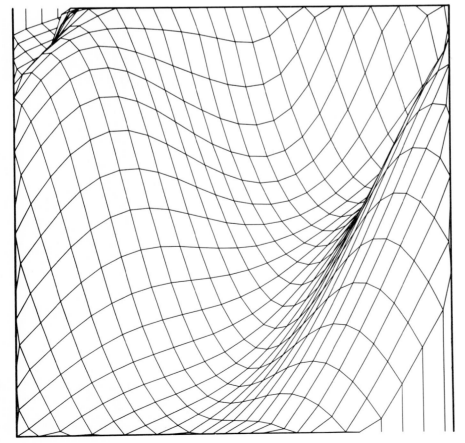

68

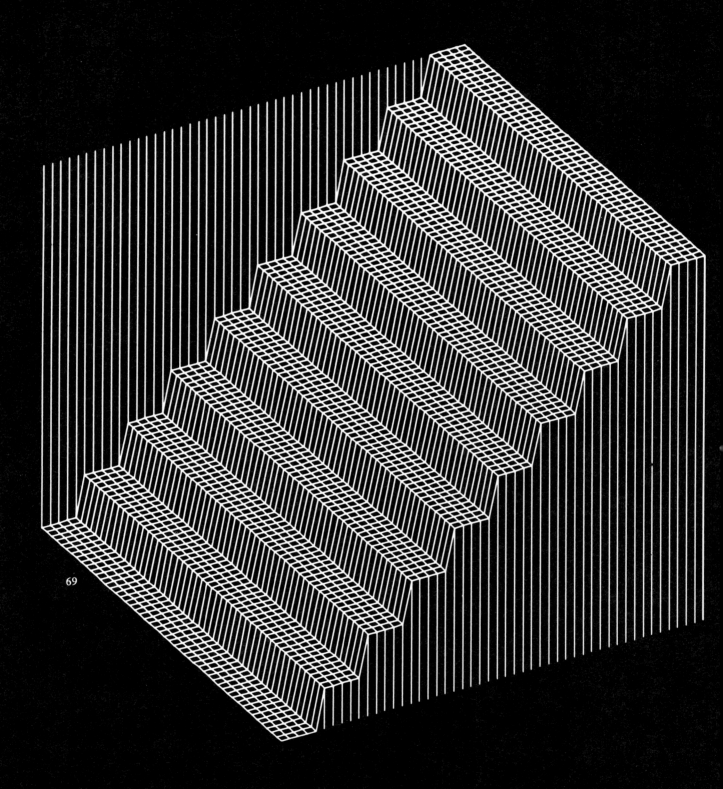

69. Optical illusion stairway. After staring at this isometric projection for a few seconds, it appears to flip upside down The brain tries to find the best orientation, but the orientation remains ambiguous.

70. When the stairway is drawn in perspective, ambiguity is removed. It is difficult to flip this figure.

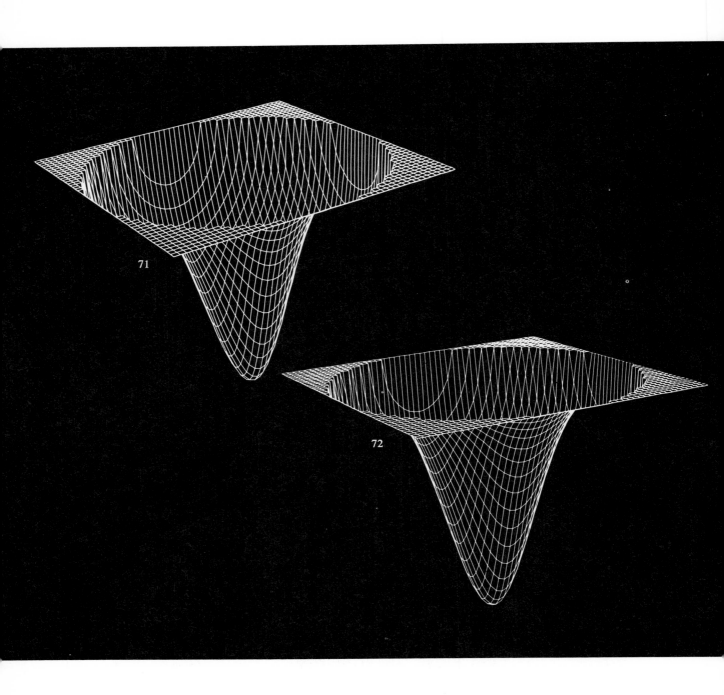

71, 72. "Bigger on the inside, smaller on the outside." These two views at different elevations of an apparent paradox were easily generated by the computer. The upper side of the surface was defined and drawn, then the surface was redefined for the bottom side.

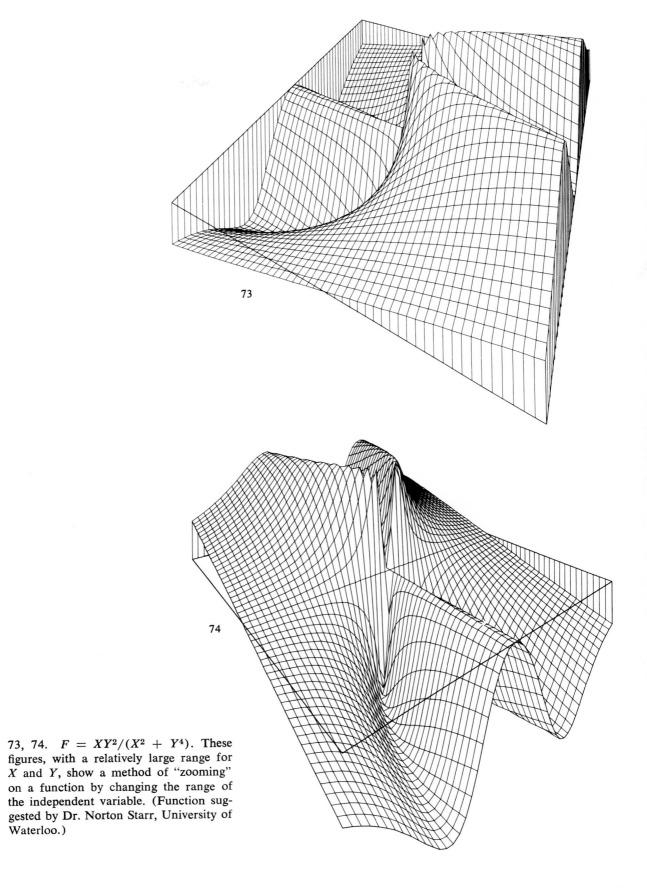

73

74

73, 74. $F = XY^2/(X^2 + Y^4)$. These figures, with a relatively large range for X and Y, show a method of "zooming" on a function by changing the range of the independent variable. (Function suggested by Dr. Norton Starr, University of Waterloo.)

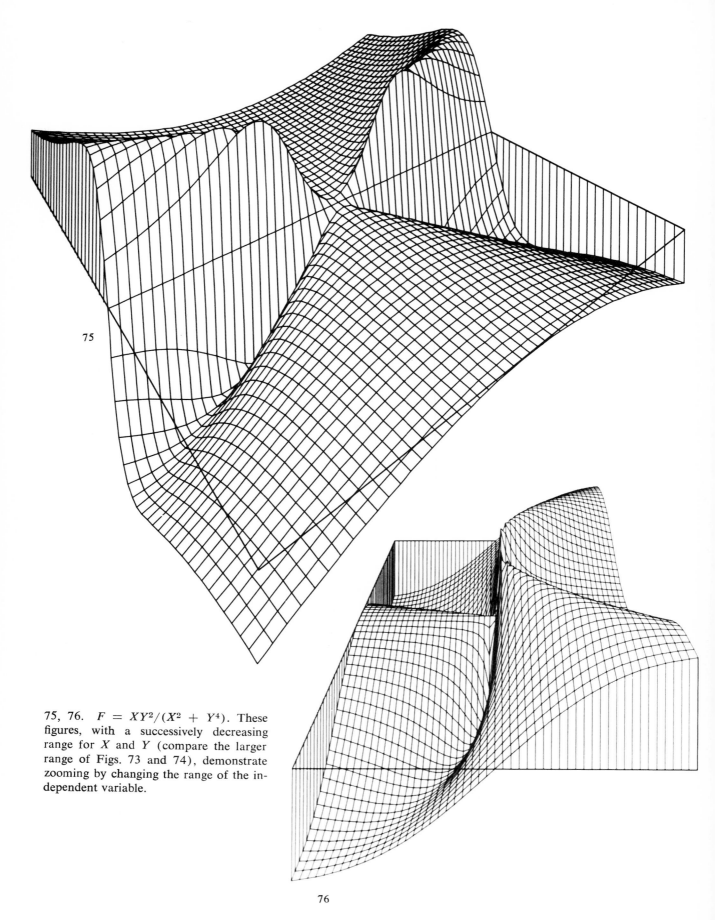

75

75, 76. $F = XY^2/(X^2 + Y^4)$. These figures, with a successively decreasing range for X and Y (compare the larger range of Figs. 73 and 74), demonstrate zooming by changing the range of the independent variable.

76

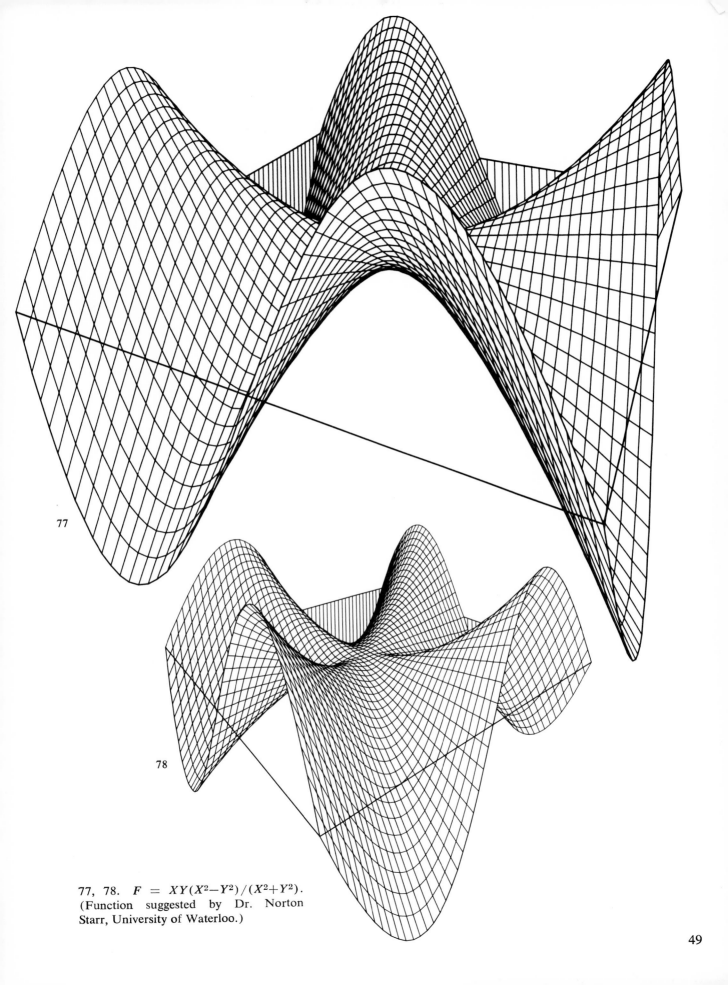

77

78

77, 78. $F = XY(X^2-Y^2)/(X^2+Y^2)$.
(Function suggested by Dr. Norton
Starr, University of Waterloo.)

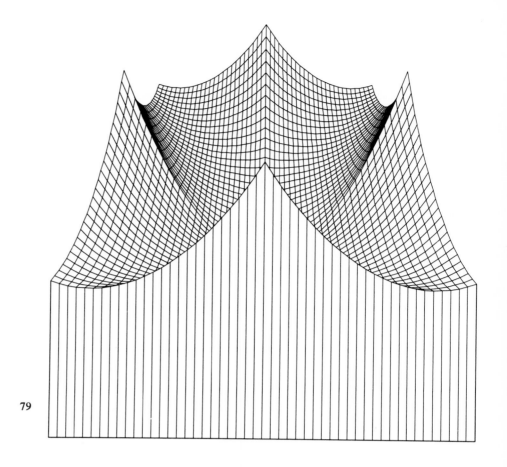

79

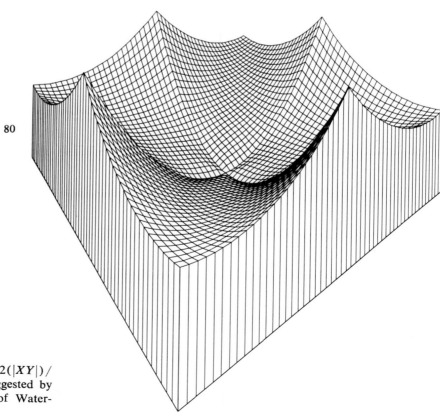

80

79, 80. $F = (|X|-|Y|)^2 + 2(|XY|)/[(X^2 + Y^2)^{1/2}]$. (Function suggested by **Dr. Norton Starr**, University of Waterloo.)

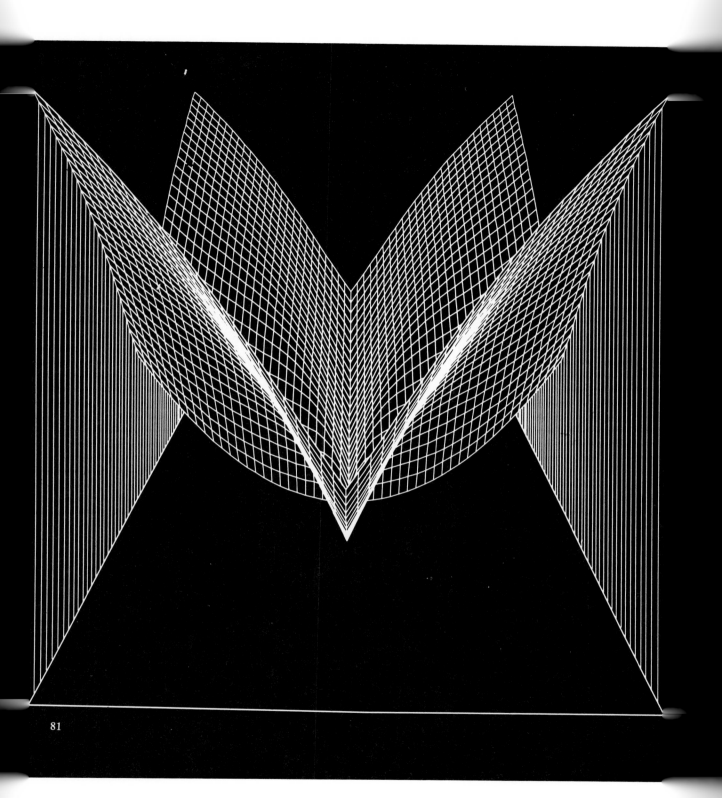

81

81. $F = (|X|-|Y|)^2 + 2(|XY|)/$
$[(X^2 + Y^2)^{1/2}]$, but the range of X and
Y is smaller than in Figures 79 and 80.

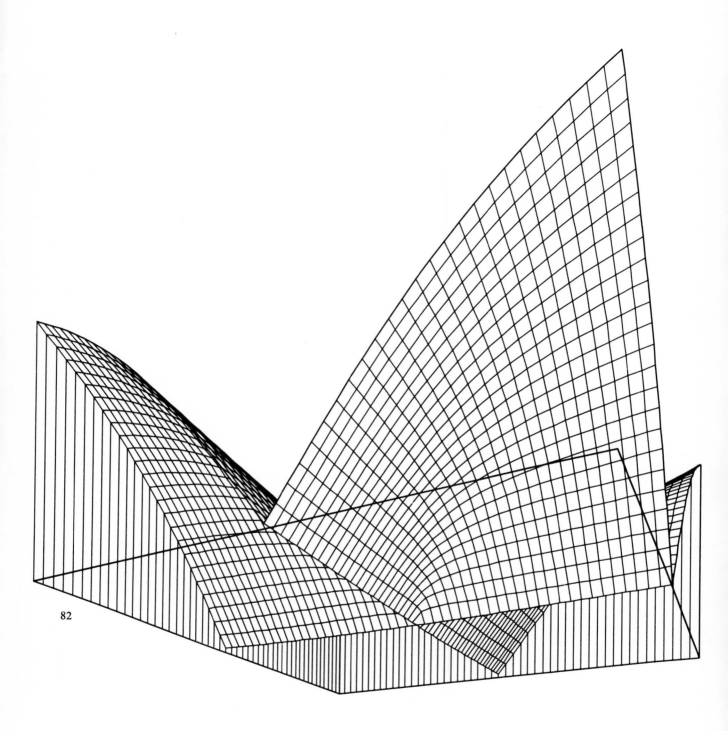

82. $F = (|X|-|Y|)^2 + 2(|XY|)/[(X^2 + Y^2)^{1/2}]$, but the range of X and Y is much smaller than in Figures 79, 80 and 81. View is from below.

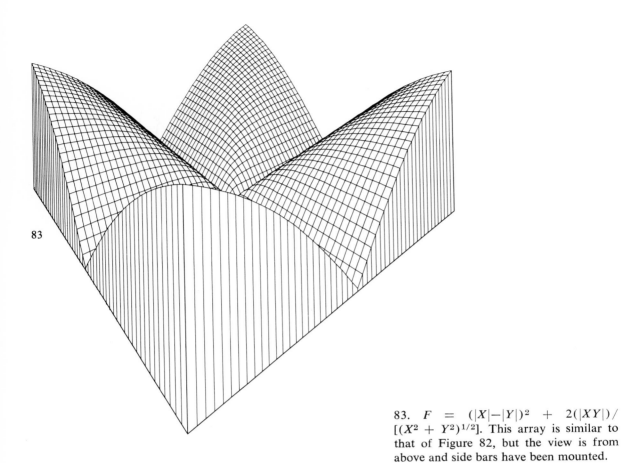

83

83. $F = (|X|-|Y|)^2 + 2(|XY|)/[(X^2 + Y^2)^{1/2}]$. This array is similar to that of Figure 82, but the view is from above and side bars have been mounted.
84. Hemisphere.

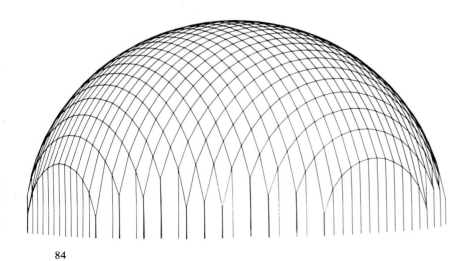

84

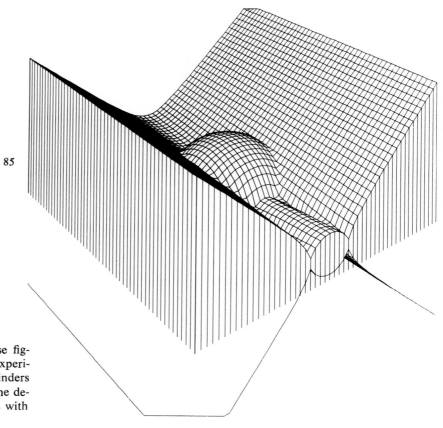

85

85–87. Experimental shapes. These figures represent designs created by experimenting with planes, spheres, cylinders and other functions. In Figure 87, the design consists of four radiating cones with side bars descending halfway.

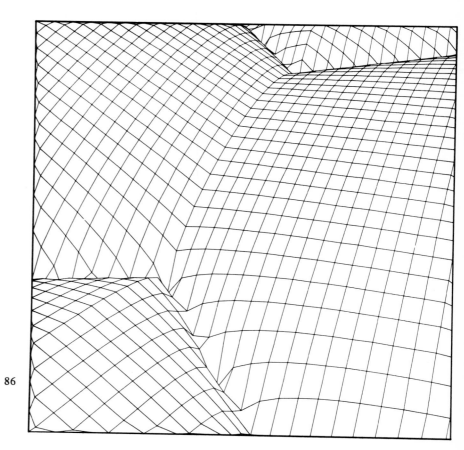

86

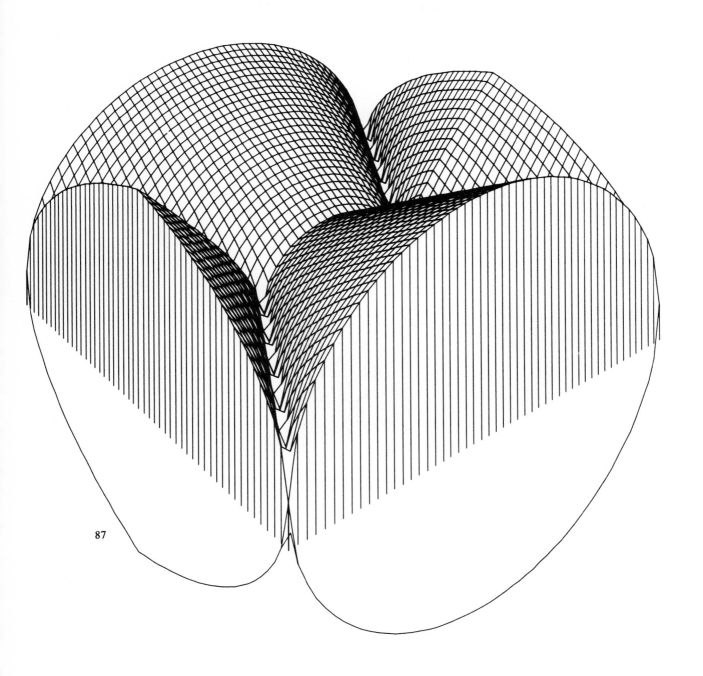

87

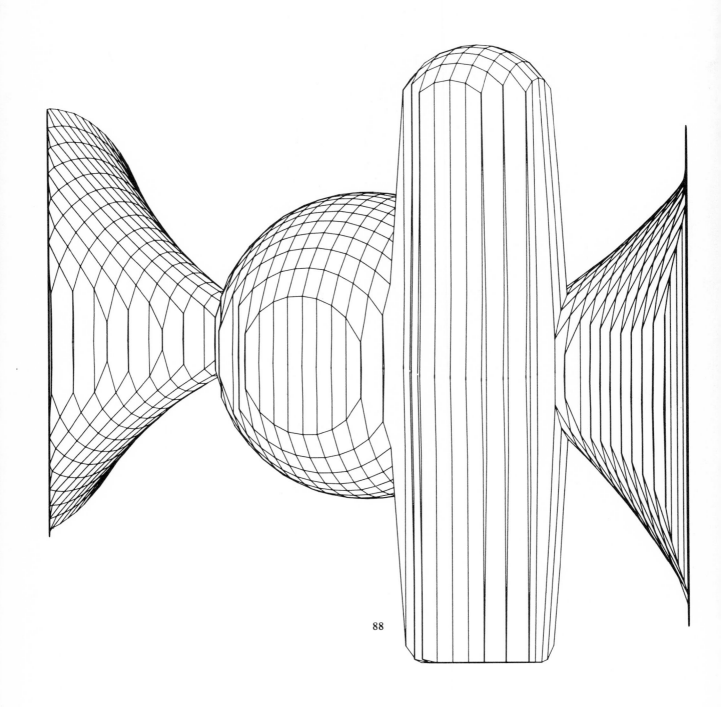

88

88–90. Experimental shapes.

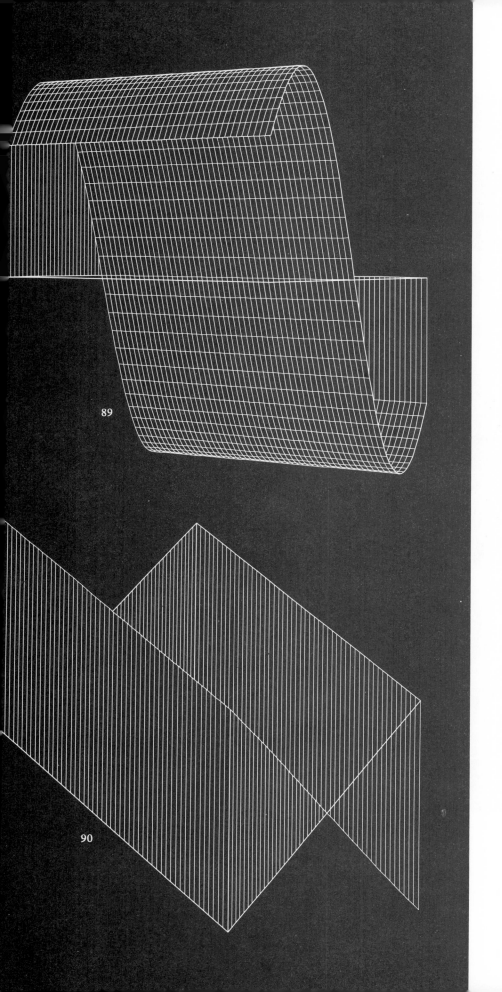

89

90

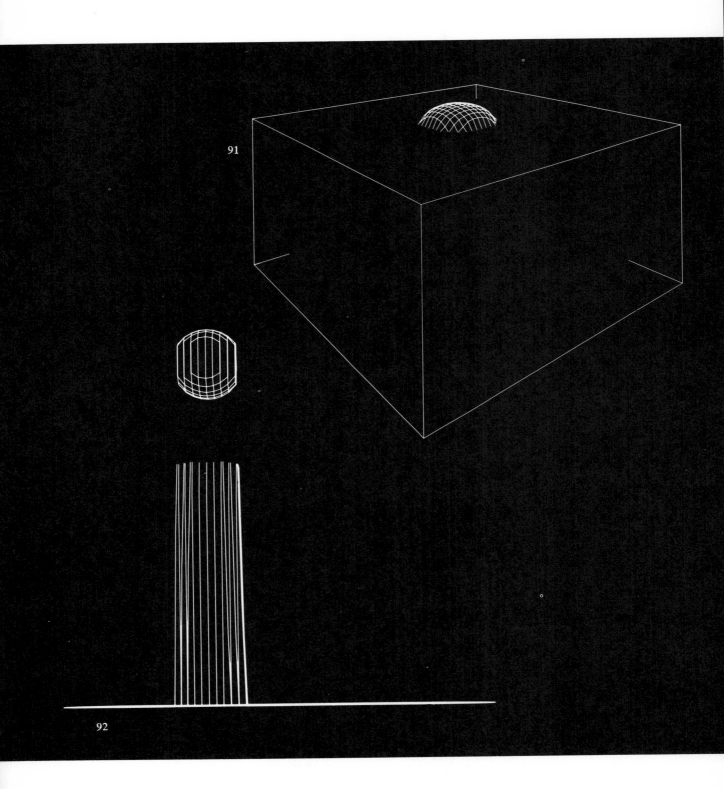

91. Hemispherical cap on a box. Most
of the image has been deleted.
92. Ball above column.

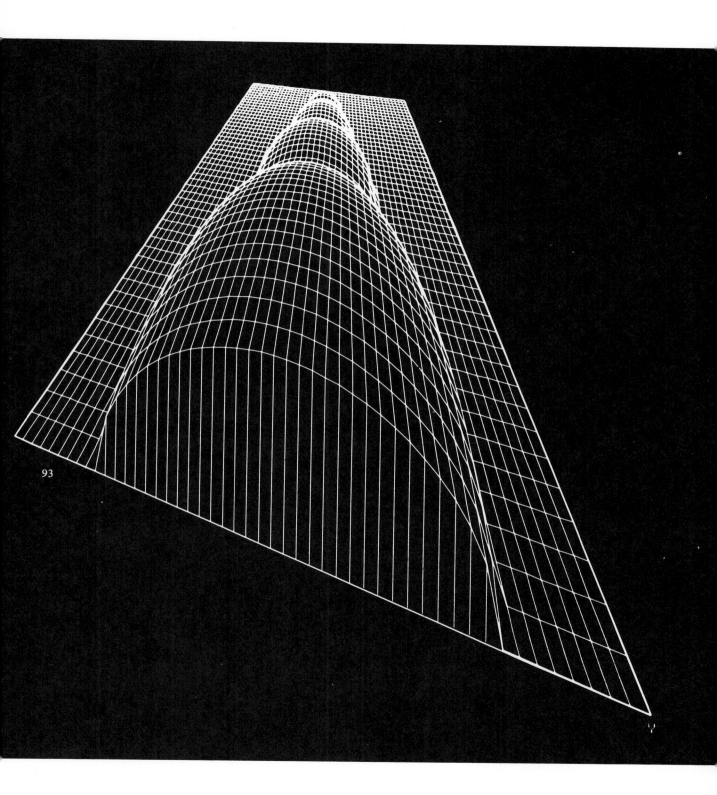

93. Distorted intersecting spheres. The distortion is caused by a very close viewpoint and by instructing the computer to make the image frame square.

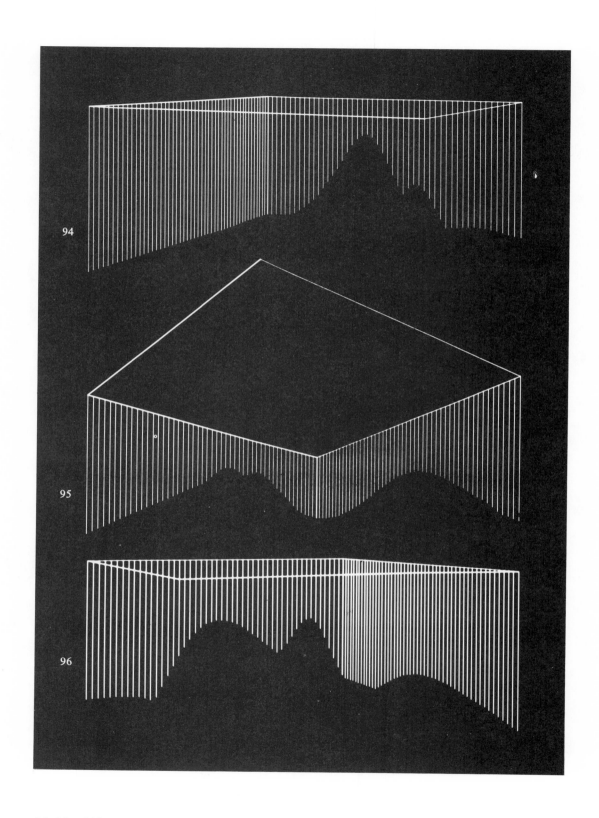

94–96. Silhouettes. Interesting shadows
are produced by plotting the side bars
without the surface.

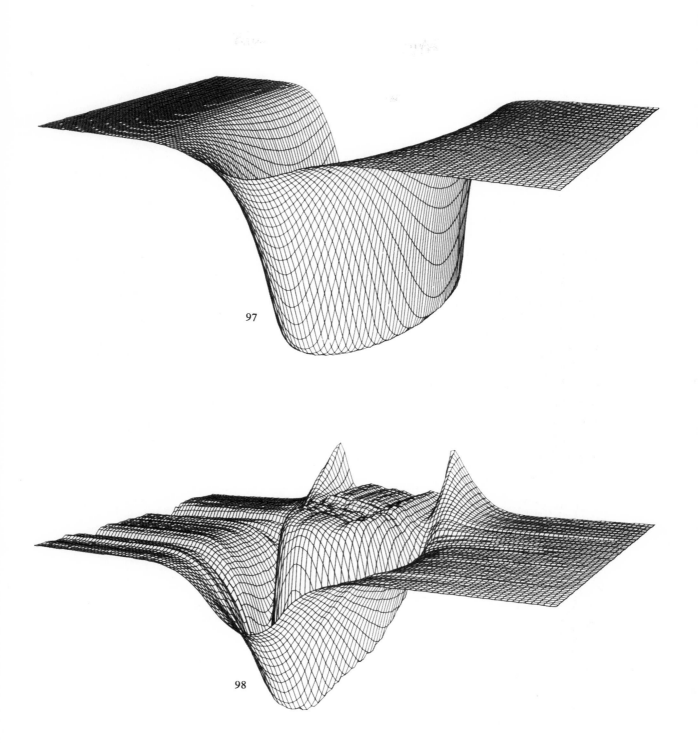

97, 98. The shape of a magnetic field. These plots of magnetic field components were made at the Los Alamos Meson Physics Facility by Dr. Gordon Lind, Professor of Physics at the Utah State University.

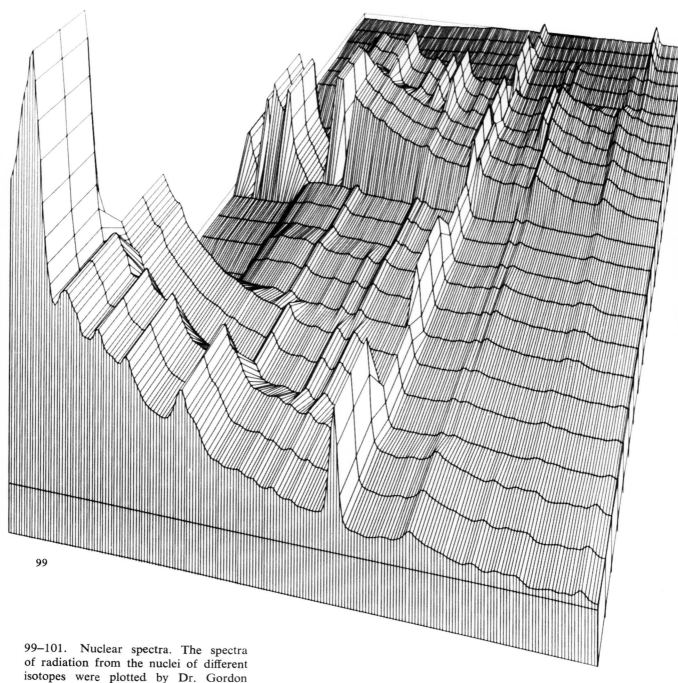

99

99–101. Nuclear spectra. The spectra
of radiation from the nuclei of different
isotopes were plotted by Dr. Gordon
Lind using the PICTURE program. Each
plot represents a different portion of the
spectrum, plotted in a slightly different
manner. Each row (running from left to
right) represents a different nucleus.
Figures 100 and 101 show the spectra of
the same nuclei as in Figure 99, but over
a different energy range.

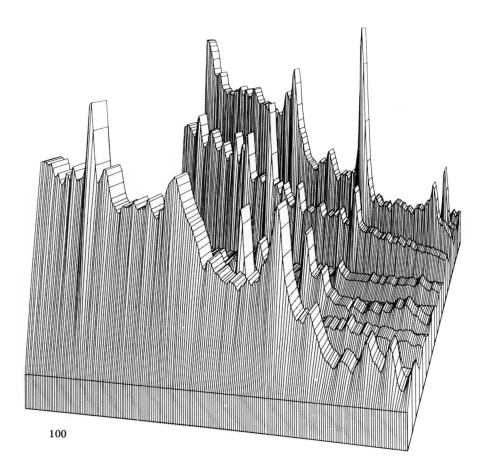

100

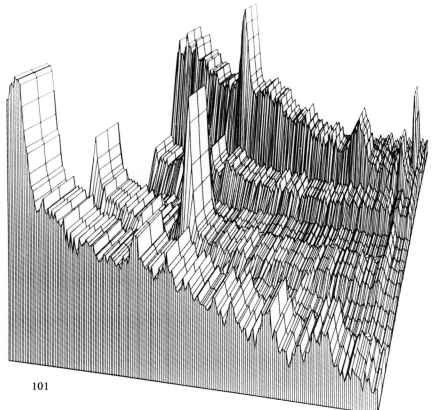

101

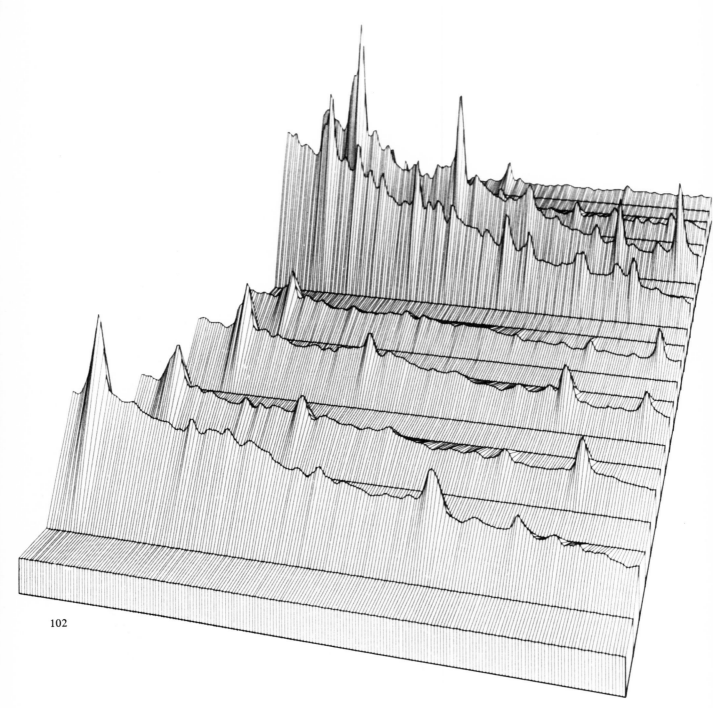

102

102. Nuclear spectrum with different energy than that in Figures 99–101 and differently displayed.

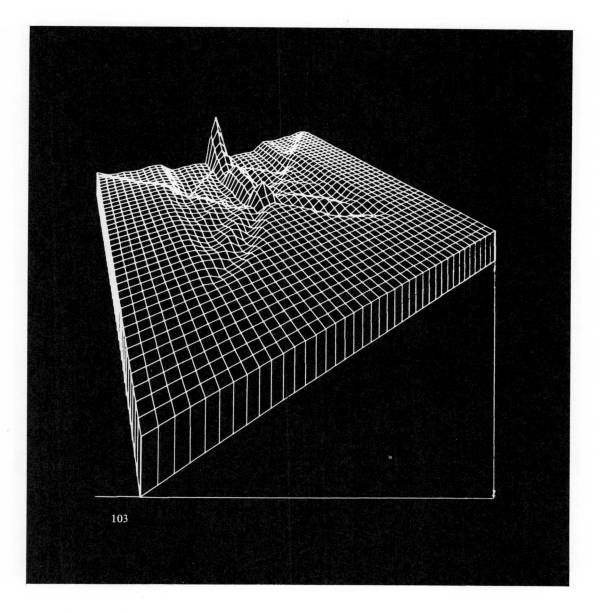

103

103. Density distribution in a molecular
dynamics problem.

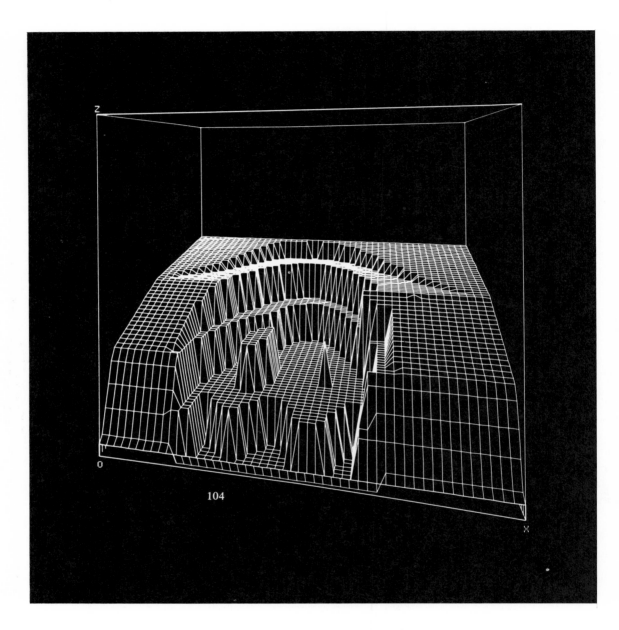

104, 105. X-ray density plots. Stan Marsh, a staff member of the Los Alamos Scientific Laboratory, plotted X-ray data of particles with PICTURE.

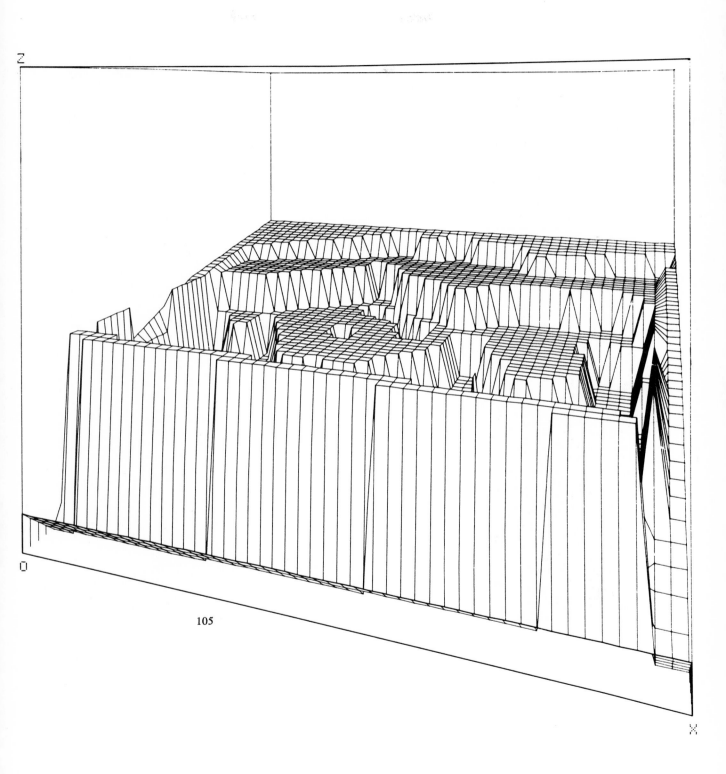

105

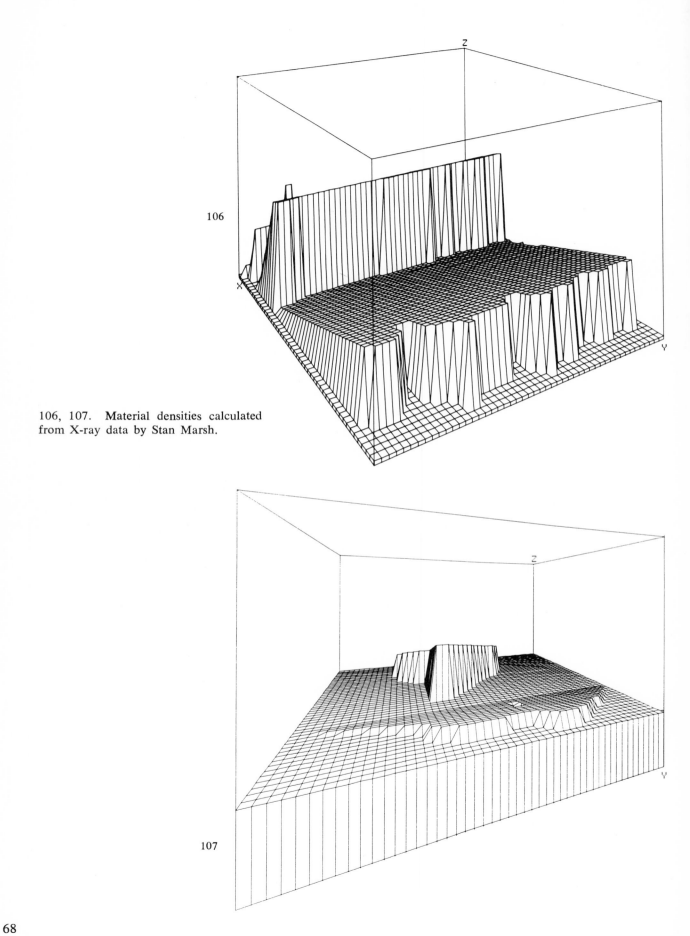

106, 107. Material densities calculated
from X-ray data by Stan Marsh.

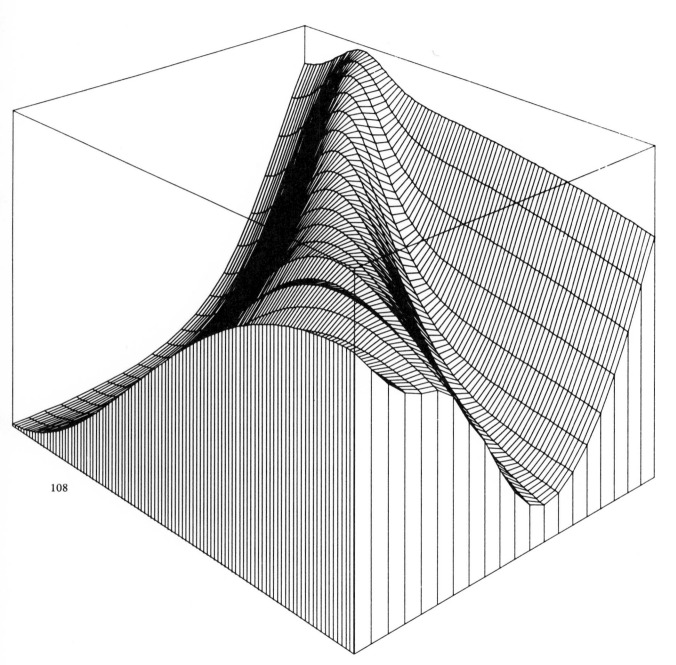

108

108. Laser absorption. Dr. Marvin M. Mueller, a staff member at the Los Alamos Scientific Laboratory, plotted absorption of laser energy (height of surface) versus angle of incidence (from left to right) and penetration depth (from front to back).